WATCHING FROM THE WINGS

Fifty Years of Working with the Stars

JIM BROCHU

For Pete, Vera and Steve

INTRODUCTION

After thirty-five years of living with Jim Brochu, the best thing I can say about him is that no matter how many times he tells his wonderful stories, I never get tired of hearing them.

He has serenaded audiences for decades with these incredible backstage escapades on Broadway stages, cabaret stages, regional theatres, cruise ships, salons and living rooms, and the audiences only clamor for more.

\Whether he's talking about growing up in Brooklyn, New York, carousing backstage and in dressing rooms at Broadway theaters sharing Kentucky Fried Chicken with Colonel Sanders and Noel Coward, witnessing the volcanic Zero Mostel turn from monster to innocent angel in a split second, or playing backgammon across the table from Lucille Ball, both of them laughing and competing like two mad dogs over a fifty-cent bet, it's all true and all so much fun.

Whenever we have a party at our Manhattan apartment or when we are visiting other people, at some point in the proceedings, everyone will quiet down and beg him to tell stories, and they will sit spellbound, waiting for the next one and the next.

But perhaps the most important aspect of this book, is that he paints a portrait of an era, the Golden Age of Broadway, as seen through the eyes of someone trying very hard to make it, sometimes living on the periphery and watching it all from the wings and sometimes taking center stage.

For people who love that world, this book will be a godsend, filling in delicious details.. For people who don't know this world, this book will be an entertaining and educational first-hand account that will, hopefully pique their curiosity to learn more. Grab a drink, settle into a comfy chair, and prepare to drift into an almost bygone world of the boy who never became the first Brooklyn born Pope, but who did find his place among the stars.

Steve Schalchlin
New York City
October 2020

CHAPTER ONE
Legends and Longitudes

March 22, 1973 - San Carlos, California

I turned around in my front row seat to watch Marlene Dietrich scurrying down the aisle past me, generating a baby blue vortex of Chanel-scented air as she sprinted toward the unlit stage of the Circle Star Theatre. Glancing over her shoulder to memorize the route she would walk down the aisle in a few hours, she noticed me sitting there alone, an audience of one in a two thousand-seat theatre, then continued to the stage counting to herself with each step. Rehearsal had begun.

"Twenty-two, twenty-thwee, twenty-four..." she muttered and then, looking straight forward, head tilted up, she used the golden tips of her sequined high heels to feel out the three steps leading to the circular stage.

She raised herself up so gracefully it was as though some invisible hand was lifting her and gently placing her back down. She was rehearsing her entrance down the steeply raked aisle and feeling out the steps for that evening's opening. As long as she was there, she'd sing a couple of songs.

I was startled - though I'm easily startled - because A) I had just smoked a joint with her stage manager in the alley next to the theatre (Yes, it was the 70s and mid-afternoon joints were mandatory) and B) I was assured that Dietrich never attended orchestra rehearsals; certainly never on her opening night; and if she did attend, she never, ever sang.

Dressed in a light blue denim pantsuit with wide bell-bottoms and tightly tailored jacket, her outfit was topped by an enormous denim Dutch boy cap perched upon unkempt tangles of ash blonde hair. With pie-plate sized sunglasses obscuring her eyes, she was heading straight for the microphone. The sparkling golden shoes were anachronistic to her blue jean ensemble but the three-inch heels were the ones she would be wearing for the performance that evening and she needed to be sure of her footing. She was not happy.

Stan Freeman, her musical director and my best friend, was conducting the orchestra and had just begun the introduction to Where Have All The Flowers Gone? which Dietrich sang as an anti-Vietnam War protest. Stanley was looking at his music when she glided unseen onto the stage behind him and he jumped a foot and stamped out his ever-present Marlborough Light when she started to bark out orders. A few of the musicians tapped their instruments as a way of acknowledging her presence but she either didn't notice or didn't care. The music continued.

"Get me a wamp! I need a wamp! With a wail! A wail I can hold onto. I can't climb steps with a spotlight in my eyes. I WANT A WAMP!" It dawned on the stoned-out stage manager that he was responsible for satisfying such a request and began darting around trying to locate a "wamp" as the work lights suddenly popped on. Although the stage would revolve a complete 360 degrees for her performance, it was stationary for now. The great Dietrich faced me as she grabbed the microphone and caught up to the song, joining in with the orchestra on "…long time passing…Where have all the flowers gone, long time ago."

Without makeup, standing under stark work lights that bleached the color from her hat, her clothes and the lines from her face, she was transfigured into a black and white image. I felt as though I was watching an early print of The Blue Angel with the film Dietrich in front of me and not a live person. She was mesmerizing. There was something so compelling about her presence that you appreciated why she had departed the rank of movie star and had arrived at the portal of living legend.

I was so taken by the sight of her that I almost forgot how cold it was in the domed cavern - what seemed a few degrees above freezing. Dietrich told us all in the limo on the ride out that she wanted the air to be glacial so that the audience would remain alert. At this temperature, they would congeal. Standing at the mike, she was singing full out,

"Where have all the graveyards gone, long time passing? Where have all the graveyards gone long time ago?" in a low rumbling monotone that made her sound more like an ancient monk chanting than a chanteuse.

Suddenly she stopped. "Whewe are de bullets? Wemember de bullets!" she admonished Stanley.

"I'll make sure they're louder, Marlene," bellowed Stan as he abruptly waved the orchestra to a stop and shouted, "At numbers 78 and 79, those violins are fortissimo and multi-pizzicato. They should sound like gunshots."

"And bullets!" added Dietrich.

The orchestra began again and the violins pierced the air with their staccato shrapnel stings as Dietrich sang on to the end of Pete Seeger's masterpiece.

She stepped back from the mic as Stan told the orchestra that the next song was, unlike Dietrich's current mood, bouncy and whimsical. It was Australian Charles Marrowood's novelty number, "Boomerang Baby." Stan started the slinky vamp and Dietrich purred into the mic.

"Boom boom-boom-boom-boom-a-wang, baby. Fly, fly away, fly away from me, you boom-a-wang baby."

When she got to the spoken bridge of the song, she took off those enormous sunglasses and looked me right in the eye, "Hey there. Back so soon? Have a nice twip?" She finished the song and asked again, to no one in particular, "Whewe is my wamp?"

The stage manager, still too stoned to move quickly, sauntered down the aisle and assured Marlene that a ramp was being taken out of storage and would be in place within fifteen minutes.

"I will not be lied to," she said with sharp finality.

Muttering something to the effect of "Everybody lies to you," the worker set off again to look for a "wamp." I recalled a story Stan told me about conducting for Dietrich during her Tokyo engagement at the Imperial Hotel when a concertmaster's lie very nearly led to an International incident.

The Japanese rehearsal was to begin at one p.m. By one-thirty, only half of the local Tokyo musicians had arrived and Dietrich asked where the other half were and why they were so late? It was "un-pwofessional! "

The concertmaster, bowing excessively low, indicated to Miss Dietrich that the string section was stuck in a massive traffic jam near the Ginza and would arrive at the venue shortly. Dietrich thought it was strange explanation and asked a very logical question, "Do they all dwive here together in one car?" The concertmaster responded with another plastic smile, more excessive bow and backed away from her without further comment.

Ten minutes more went by when Dietrich encountered the first violinist and asked him where the other musicians were?

"They called in sick," he told her, "and the producers were finding substitutes." Another bow.

Stan reported that Dietrich went ballistic. She drove her foot through the floorboard of political correctness and shattered it by saying, "Stop! I have now been told two diffewent stowies. First, the musicians are delayed by twaffic and now you tell me they are all sick. This is not acceptable. You have pwoven to me once and for all that the Japanese are sneaking, thieving, lying little people and I have not forgotten Pearl Harbor!" Marlene was not going to get an Ambassadorship to Tokyo that year.

Stan said there was a party for her after the opening show given by the Mayor of Tokyo where extravagant golden-silk kimonos had been made specially to present to her as gifts. She was so upset by the lies she had been told that she refused to attend and sent word to the Mayor "to take back his bathwobes!"

I was snapped out of my daydream by a change of lighting. Some techies noticed Dietrich on the stage, turned out the house lights, brought the stage lights up and a phenomenon occurred. She seemed to get taller in the light, like a flower responding to the sun as she let them warm and comfort her. She stepped back and listened for the introduction to the next song. It was "I Wish You Love."

I wondered why I had smoked that joint with the stage manager outside in the alley before rehearsals began. Was I appreciating the full impact of this event? Again, it was 1973 and everyone smoked pot for breakfast with their coffee and I thought the music would sound enhanced. The fact that Dietrich herself was singing to me alone in the middle of this icy cavern was by far the most surrealistic experience of my life to date.

Yes, this moment with Dietrich was it. Especially as she stopped singing in the middle of the song when she saw that a ramp had just been exchanged for the three steps and Dietrich seemed eager to try it out. She hit the aisle and just as she passed me, said, "The Fisherman" and kept on going. It sounded like code -- something one spy would say to another before exposing all their secrets.

"The Fisherman." She didn't really stop. She didn't really look directly at me, yet I knew she was speaking to me and wanted a response. But I was still too stoned to comprehend her meaning or form a response. "The Fisherman?" What did it all mean? Was there a clandestine operation going on?

I thought about Myron Cohen's joke about the Jewish spy on his first day at the job. He's given the most dangerous and critical assignment in the history of the CIA. He is to go to an address, ring the doorbell marked "GOLDBERG"
and when a man comes to the door, say the code: "The Sun Is Shining." He will then be given confidential documents that will save the world. If anything goes wrong he is to bite down on a cyanide capsule placed under his tongue. At all costs, this mission must be kept top secret.

Our new spy gets to the address and sees two names and two buzzers: A. GOLDBERG (1-A) and R. GOLDBERG (2-A). He rings the first bell and an elderly man comes to the door. The new spy says, "The sun is shining." The old man says "You want Goldberg, the Spy - Upstairs." So Dietrich is the spy and "The Fisherman" is the code. Jeez, that pot was good.

After the rehearsal, Stan solved the mystery by reporting Marlene had invited everyone in her party out to dinner at a restaurant in San Francisco called The Fisherman after that evening's show. Since I was with him, I was part of the group. The show would start in four hours and since we were an hour drive from San Francisco, we brought a change of clothes and would shower in the dressing room. Stanley thought that Dietrich was in a particularly good mood since she had deigned to come to the rehearsal.

"She wanted to try out her wamp," I explained, "and she decided to stay. She saw me sitting there and wanted to do it just for me." Stanley laughed -- God what an easy and wonderful laugher he was. His voice was like stone workers sifting through a gravel pit but when he laughed, his eyes completely shut and a rumble of contagious guffaws burst forth.

When I went to San Francisco with him for this engagement, we had been friends for four years, having met through my roommate at the time, Bob Nigro, who directed the long-gone CBS soap opera, "Search For Tomorrow." Bobby was another great laugher with a hairline trigger for high tone giggles that lasted forever. One of the greatest laughs the three of us ever had was at Bobby's expense.

We were at Stan's house on Fire Island when Bobby walked directly into a closed floor-to-ceiling plate-glass door and knocked himself unconscious. Stanley and I were still hysterical when he came around. We weren't being mean. Bobby had commented not an hour before that only an idiot couldn't tell the difference between that door being opened and being closed.

The forty-five minute trip from San Francisco to San Carlos was taken in a stretch limo with the passengers being Miss Dietrich, Stanley, myself, Jeanette (Marlene's aide de camp), Gene (her drummer) and Gene's wife, who was also one of Marlene's helpers. It was a stretch limo that featured jump seats and could hold five comfortably. Marlene opted to sit up front with the driver and leave the six of us fighting over the five seats.

Jeanette met us at the top of the aisle and told us that Marlene was taking a nap but she would see us all at seven-thirty for cocktails. Stan said La Dietrich always had a few people in her dressing room an hour before the show and served champagne, which she never took herself. It was all part of the ritual.

We stayed in Stan's dressing room with Chinese take-out until it was time to change and go to Marlene's.

The drummer and his wife were there already along with Joe Davies (her British lighting designer), Jeff (the stoned stage manager), the owner of the theatre and his wife, and a silent, dazed-looking girl who just stood there without any seeming affiliation.

We thought Marlene was in the other room of her dressing room suite, but then Jeanette came in from the hallway, followed by Marlene who had changed into a
bright red tailored pantsuit, white blouse and red fedora.

"Well, it looks like a pawty," she said, "But what is a pawty without champagne." The theatre owner signaled the silent girl who went to the hallway and returned with a liquor trolley. Jeanette had already opened the door to the inner room and from where I sat, I could see Marlene's famous nude dress in the mirror.

It looked like it was standing up by itself. Marlene, looking older than her 70+ years, hung on the door of the inner room for a moment with a knowing smile on her face. She looked like a magician about to enter the enchanted box, and only she held the secret of the trick. The dressing room door closed and the old woman disappeared.

Remember Houdini's great illusion, The Metamorphosis? He would lock his assistant in a trunk upon which he would then stand. A curtain flew up, then down and in an instant they changed places and Houdini emerged from the trunk in a totally different costume. Forty-five minutes later, when Dietrich's dressing room door opened and she stepped back into the room, she had been completely transformed into the icon-legend-megastar of the Silver Screen. She was breathtaking. None of us could speak as we all took her in. Then she broke the ice. "Anybody have a banana?"

Speaking of magic tricks, Jeanette seemed to pull a banana out of thin air and handed it to Marlene who carefully pulled the skin back and admired it before taking a bite off the end. I asked, "Do you always have a banana before a show, Marlene?"

"Always!" she told me. "Potassium!" And I'll have another at intermission. It's good for when you have to stand so long."

"Fifteen minutes, Miss Dietrich!" announced Jeff, the Stage Manager. Joe Davies raised his champagne, "To our Marlene!"

I wondered if I should join in the toast. After all, I had only met her the day before at the airport and wasn't sure if I knew her well enough to enjoin with the others to drink to "Our Marlene." But I lifted my glass. "To Our Marlene!" After all, she was everyone's Marlene.

As soon as the toast was done, Jeanette opened the door to escort us out. Marlene turned to the mirror and began to study every inch of herself as the door closed like a wipe fading out on a scene from one of her old movies. We stepped through the curtain into the back of the arena, which was packed and buzzing with anticipation.

I walked down the same aisle I saw Dietrich stroll down that afternoon and I started counting my steps. I stopped at twenty-four. It was twenty-eight steps to the ramp. I sat in the second row with Joe Davies, the designer who created the magical lighting that kept her looking like a Rembrandt for two hours.

Stanley came down the aisle in his tuxedo, unannounced and unlit. He was wearing a new toupee. It was a little too big for his head. I had noticed at the orchestra rehearsal that his hair had seemed to have edema. It was at least twice as big as it had been when he woke up that morning. His appointment to get a "haircut" had been actually to get a new hairpiece that was styled with bangs and wings that reminded me of Imogene Coca. This one was so oversized you could, as they say, "Get to Baghdad on that rug!" The day after Dietrich opened at the Circle Star, the review in the San Francisco Chronicle was a rave except they reported that "Miss Dietrich's conductor looked like Peter Lorre with a bad toupee."

When Stan was in place on the stage, the house lights went out, the audience fluttered and a spotlight cut through the dark from one side of the arena to the other.

"Ladies and gentlemen, the one and only, Marlene Dietrich." Stan raised his hand and the orchestra came to life with the horns trumpeting the first notes of *Falling In Love Again,* much like heralders announcing the arrival of a queen.

Wearing that incredible white ermine coat which followed behind her like a white wolf clinging to her ankles, she stepped into her beam and floated down the aisle, looking straight forward, neither waving to the cheering crowd nor acknowledging the standing ovation they were giving her. Head high, moving forward, I applauded her and chuckled to myself that I was the only one there who knew what was going on in her head - she was counting the steps.

On the twenty-eighth step she started to ascend the "wamp" and the crowd exploded. She walked the perimeter of the circular stage so that everyone, as Ethel Mertz might say, could get a load of her. She acknowledged Stanley and stepped to the mic and purred into it as if it were the ear of her great paramour.

"I can't give you anything but love, baby.
That's the only thing I've plenty of, baby..."

After two more songs, the coat came off, the stage turned, she sang two dozen more songs including *Lili Marlene* and *Falling In Love Again* and left them wanting more. The audience stood and screamed.

I had seen this same show twice before Stan and I ever met. Once was in Montreal during Expo '67 and also when she played the Lunt-Fontanne on Broadway. I took my cousin Eileen Quain to see it and she begged me to wait with her so we could get Dietrich's autograph after the show. We stood outside the stage door in three-degree weather, right next to the door, and when Dietrich came out my cousin thrust her program at her, "Miss Dietrich, may I please have your autograph?" implored Eileen.

Without even looking at her, Dietrich said "No" and pushed her way through the crowd to her waiting limo. Oh, well. Five years later, I wanted to call Eileen and tell her I was sitting with Dietrich in her dressing room after her show drinking champagne with her but she wouldn't believe me. I hardly believed it myself.

"I'm vewy hungwy," said Marlene, who had now switched to vodka. "We're going to the Fisherman. I have a cwaving for soft-shelled cwabs."

Stanley bellowed, "How about you, Jim? Some soft-shelled crabs and then scallops and maybe shrimp cocktail, lobster and shad roe? How does that sound?"

I raised my glass and returned his toast by sticking out my tongue at him, which Marlene caught.

"What's this?"

Stan explained that he was kidding with me because I had an aversion to fish. I couldn't stand the sight of it. (Still can't.) I tried to eat tuna salad once and couldn't actually come to put it in my mouth before I started gagging. I know it's totally psychological. I know it's totally irrational. I know I'm depriving myself of some of the greatest culinary pleasures on earth. But I hate fish and will never eat it.

Stan finished explaining my "problem" to Marlene and why he was laughing. Marlene looked at me very strangely.

"No fish?" she asked.

"No fish," I echoed.

The deep-seated aversion I had to fish was inexplicable. I had grown up less than a quarter of a mile from New York Harbor, in Bay Ridge which is the section of Brooklyn that anchors the Verrazano Bridge. For the first ten years of my life a squat, green ferry crossed the narrows from the 69th street pier in Bay Ridge to Staten Island. The ferry went out of business when the bridge was finished in 1964, but the pier at 69th street was a favorite fishing spot where all the neighbors would go crabbing on the weekends.

I was terrified by the sight of these mesh cages filled with living breathing, ugly, monstrous crabs. My uncle John would be one of the fishermen from time to time and would take the crabs out of their cages and chase after me aiming the crabs for my throat. I had also just seen The Creature From The Black Lagoon which didn't help my paranoia about biting into things that lived under the water.

In the Joan of Arc nursery school, one of the teachers tried to convince me that the tuna salad she was serving me was actually chicken, but after one taste I knew I had been lied to and became hysterical. Fish and I would never come to an easy agreement.

Dietrich picked up the phone in her dressing room and dialed 411. "Get me The Fisherman," she purred. Obviously, the operator didn't realize it was the great Marlene Dietrich when she asked. "What city please?"

"I don't know what city, just connect me to The Fisherman. It's an expensive fish westauwant."

She held the receiver for a moment while the operator found the number and then made the connection.

"Hello, Fisherman?"

I swear I thought she was going to cut the reservation to seven instead of eight and let me sit in the car while they all had dinner. Instead she said, "This is Marlene Dietrich speaking. I am coming to your westauwant with a party of eight. One of my guests eats no fish. Does the Fisherman serve meat?" It sounded like
an oxymoron. A meat-catching fisherman. She listened for a moment then nodded as though she

understood the answer and hung up. "There will be no problem. Shall we go?"

It only took her a few minutes to change into her red pants suit and we left by the stage door. There was a crowd of about twenty waiting for an autograph or just a close up look at the great star, but she was like a tight end pushing her way through the people, not stopping, not looking until she was inside the back of the limo. The rest of us followed her in and within a few minutes we were being escorted into The Fisherman. The place smelled of fish.

The maître d' bowed and led us to a beautifully set round table in the corner overlooking the wharf. Most of the people in her entourage didn't want to sit next to her, leaving me next to the legend who still looked like the icon rather than the old German lady. As soon as we got settled, Stan Freeman noticed a young girl approaching the table. She was heading straight for Dietrich. There was another great star eating at the restaurant that night and she had sent the girl over to say hello to Marlene on her behalf.

The girl pulled up right next to Dietrich and said, "Excuse me, Miss Dietrich." Without turning or looking, Marlene said loudly and coldly, "You are _not_ excused." The girl went white but persisted with her mission. "But I have regards for you from Ann Miller. She's sitting over there." Dietrich looked across the room to see Miss Miller waving to her then turned to the girl and said, "Ann who?"

"Ann Miller," repeated the girl. We all looked over to see Miss Miller waving and trying to indicate that she wanted to come over herself and join us. Dietrich was having none of it. In the hierarchy of stars in The Fisherman that night, Dietrich clearly outranked Miller.

"Well, you are vewy wude," she told Miller's emissary, "Now please leave this table."

The girl, almost in tears, ran back to the Miller table and whispered into Ann's ear. Miss Miller shrugged and everything went back to normal. Stars and public figures can be funny about fans interrupting their dinner. There's a famous story about Rex Harrison having dinner with Moss Hart at Sardi's between a matinee and evening performance of "My Fair Lady."

Legend has it that an elderly woman approached the Great Rex with a program in hand. "Oh, Mr. Harrison," she gushed, "you are my most favorite actor in the world. I've seen every film you've ever made, I waited a year for front row seats to the show and there you were in person and I was breathing the same air you were breathing and you are so handsome and talented and if only you'd sign my program my life would be complete."

Harrison turned on the lady and barked, "How dare you, you old biddy. Can't you see I'm trying to enjoy my dinner without you prattling on. I don't care who you love or what air you breathe or anything else. You are disturbing me. Now get the hell away from my table!" With that, the lady hauled off, smacked him on the head with her playbill and walked away. Moss Hart then observed, "Well, that's the first time I ever saw the fan hit the shit."

I also saw Pearl Bailey treat a young fan terribly. It was at Sardi's after a performance of *Hello, Dolly!* when a small boy of about ten approached the star at her table. "I saw the show today," said the lad, "and could I have your autograph?"

Miss Bailey sneered at the boy, "Can't you see I'm eating with my friends. Haven't your parents taught you any manners? I'll sign the program when I finish eating and you can just stand there until I do." The boy started to cry and stood frozen, not knowing what to do. His mother ran over and collected him while Miss Bailey never looked up again.

Back at The Fisherman the mood of the dinner changed for the good when Joe Davies, Dietrich's lighting designer, arrived with an early edition of the San Francisco Chronicle that contained a rave review: "Dietrich and her act are the most remarkable feat of theatrical engineering since the invention of the revolving stage, and age has if anything reinforced her voice to the point where (for *Lili Marlene* or Seeger's *Where Have All the Flowers Gone*?) she seems to have within her the strength of entire armies."

While we sat at dinner, I asked Marlene how Stan had come to be her musical director. She told me that when she first put the act together, Bewt Bachwach was her conductor and friend, but he had tired of doing the show and was preparing his first (and only) Broadway musical *Promises, Promises*. As things are meant to happen, Stan was walking down Fifth Avenue one night and ran into Bert who said Marlene was looking for a new conductor and he would recommend Stanley if he wanted the job.

Burt warned him that she wasn't easy to work with, but Stan couldn't pass up the money and the perks that came along with the job, so he took on the assignment.

The first few weeks were rocky. Stan said she was impossible to work with and found fault with everything he suggested or did. After one performance in London, Marlene complained about something Stan had done and he hit the ceiling, calling her every name in the book. He told her she couldn't sing and that she was overrated and a supreme pain in the ass to work with. She loved him from then on.

The outburst did the trick. Marlene cried and said that she couldn't lose him because he was the best conductor she had ever had. They were together for twelve years until Stanley helped to end her career for good.

They were performing at the Shady Grove Music Theatre outside Washington, D.C. On the first night, all went well except for the curtain call. Marlene came over to the foot of the stage and reached down to shake Stan's hand after the performance. He said that she had to bend so far that he was afraid she would fall into the pit.

The next night, November 14, 1973, the show went along fine -- full house, responsive crowd and standing ovation at the bow. Stan, being a gentleman, decided to stand on the piano bench so that Marlene wouldn't have to reach down as far to shake his hand. He stood on the bench, took Marlene's hand, the bench broke and he pulled her into the pit. Miss Dietrich landed on the drums, accompanying her fall with a tremendous, unexpected rim shot. Blood poured over her famous gown and it turned out she had gashed her leg open as she was impaled on the cymbal.

He told me that the audience let out a group gasp and an elderly married couple who had been sitting in the first row leaned over the orchestra pit railing and very nonplussed said, "Very nice show." An ambulance took the seventy-two-year-old to the local hospital where she was stitched up but the doctor found it difficult to close the whole wound which was about four inches in diameter. Senator Ted Kennedy sent his own personal physician to assess her condition and he told her that she lost a great deal of skin which had been sliced off by the edge of the drum kit.

Stan visited her in the hospital and was truly heartbroken that he had been the cause of her troubles. She said she didn't blame him. It was an accident and accidents happen. Though she did mention that the pain was unbearable and she would have to go through months of skin grafts and physical therapy. She added that the doctors weren't sure if the wound would ever heal or that she would ever walk properly again but that Stan shouldn't give it a second thought because it wasn't his fault - though if he hadn't gotten on the bench, the accident wouldn't have happened.

For weeks after the accident, Marlene would send pictures of her leg with horrific pictures of her wound - before and after the skin grafts - and then with huge bandages that covered her legendary leg from ankle to knee. With each note and each picture, Dietrich underscored that it wasn't his fault and he shouldn't feel guilty about it. She performed two weeks later in Toronto against her doctor's wishes where she saw no one outside of her group, traveled by freight elevator between her room and the stage and played the entire two-hour show in enormous pain. Her leg would not heal if she kept up the schedule so she knew she had to tend to her leg or it would be amputated. The leg that once had been insured by Lloyds of London.

After Toronto, Marlene returned to her apartment in Paris where Stan would call her from time to time to cheer her up. Marlene always answered the phone herself but insisted she was the maid and that Miss Dietrich couldn't come to the phone but she would pass on his good wishes.

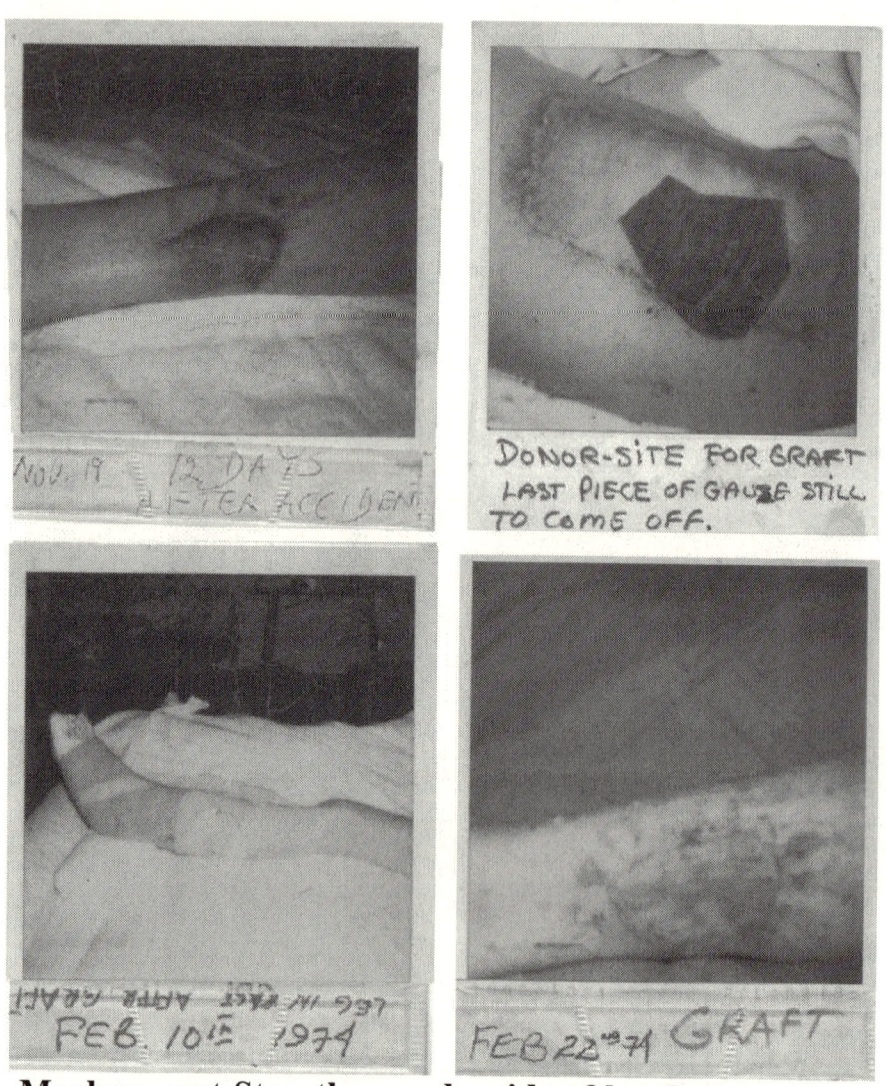

Marlene sent Stan these polaroids of her leg stressing how painful it was but that he shouldn't feel guilty.

Dietrich eventually went back to work after about nine months of recuperation and brought Stan back to conduct for her. But she wasn't the same. She was brittle and in pain while she performed and took to using a stool so that she wouldn't have to stand. Even the potassium from the bananas couldn't help. On October 4, 1975, while she was performing in Sydney, Australia she fell again without any help from Stanley and broke her leg. That was the end of her career. She never performed again and she retired to her Paris apartment, a place she never left until she was carried out feet first in 1994.

How does a kid from the Bay Ridge section of Brooklyn go into show business and get to watch Marlene Dietrich rehearse when all he ever wanted to be was a priest? I was born on August 16, 1946 in the first year of the baby boom, the second year of the Truman presidency, the third printing of Dr. Spock's The Common-Sense Book of Baby and Child Care, the fourth sold-out month of *Annie Get Your Gun* and the fifth week that "I'm Chiquita Banana" tied with "Zip-a-de-Doodah" in the top slot on *Your Hit Parade*.

Just about everyone in my family -- mother, father, grandmother, grandfather, uncle and some cousins -- were born in August which led me to believe that the Brochu-Condon-Ryan-Morrissey clans only had sex at Thanksgiving, whether they wanted to or not. They were all so logy from all that turkey that they fell into bed and did what came naturally. My father's side of the family came from French Canada by way of upstate New York and settled in Washington Heights, just south of the

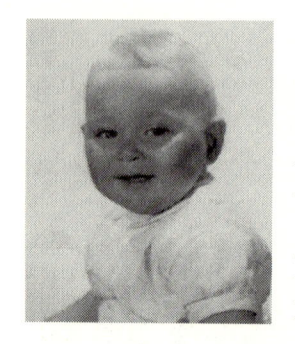

George Washington Bridge. My maternal grandmother's folks were from Ireland and settled in what was then called the Fourth Ward of New York City's lower Manhattan, an area along the East River just South of the Brooklyn Bridge. My mother, Veronica, was an only child, the daughter of Dick Condon and Theresa Morrissey: my father -- son of Joseph Brochu and Mary Ryan -- was the oldest of three boys and a girl, who died of cholera, when she was four.

Mom met dad when she worked in the steno pool for the Wall Street brokerage firm, Allen and Company, where dad was an up and coming executive. He started as a runner there in 1933 where the patriarch of the Allen clan, Charles Allen, saw potential in my father and promoted him to Municipal Bond trader.

He became enormously successful by raising bond revenues for projects such as the Mackinac Bridge in Michigan, the Brooklyn Battery Tunnel and the Verrazano Narrows Bridge.

Mother was, as my father described her, a "classy broad" who looked like Merle Oberon and enjoyed a dirty joke with the best of them. They were engaged in 1937 but didn't marry until 1943 while dad was on leave from his navy duty in the South Pacific. They pulled the wedding together in five days. My mother was never a well woman. She had a weak heart from having fought a bout of rheumatic fever when she was a child. She died on Father's Day, 1949 at the age of twenty-nine, two months short of my third birthday.

My maternal grandparents decided that they should raise me and informed my father that I would be living with them. Dad called his brother, my Uncle Bill, and together they arrived at my grandparents' apartment with the intention of beating them up if they didn't turn me over. Dick and "The Chief" backed down immediately but I always sensed a tension between them though I didn't know why for years. But when I turned seven, Dad allowed them to take me to the Poconos for a week where I had the first silly trauma of my life…but it shaped my future in a very negative way.

I was working on a jigsaw puzzle with a girl my age who was also staying at the resort. When we finished the puzzle she was so excited that she thought it should be framed. I, on the other hand thought it would be fun to mix it all up and start again. There was nothing else to do. So when the girl came back into the house to show everyone our great accomplishment and saw the puzzle undone she screamed, yelled and carried on that someone had destroyed her work. I was petrified and hid in the bathroom so I wouldn't have to face a terrible punishment.

After about an hour of hiding people started to look for me and were very worried that I had been abducted. When they finally pounded on the bathroom door, I opened it crying my eyes out. My grandmother Tessie assured me I wasn't in trouble and everything was fine. Still, it instilled in me a method I would use often when faced with a terrible situation – run and hide.

My father's widowed mother, Minnie Ryan, moved Brooklyn with her youngest son, my Uncle John, to live with us in Bay Ridge. The last thing a 60 year old woman wanted to do was take care of a three year old boy, but she made the sacrifice. The only thing she and my mother's mother Tess, who I called "Ma" but everyone else referred to as "The Chief," had in common was their devotion to the Catholic Church and the opportunity to mold me into being a priest. And it almost worked.

Like a liturgical career, I started as an altar boy and worked my way up to be our pastor, Bishop Edmond J. Reilly's personal altar boy. The Bishop formed an alliance with my grandmothers by giving me the prime daily masses and making sure I watched Bishop Fulton J. Sheen instead of Milton Berle on Tuesday nights at nine. In fact when Bishop Reilly died in 1958, Bishop Sheen came to Our Lady of Angels in Bay Ridge to deliver the eulogy and I was assigned to carry his bags. Sheen was one of my idols but at age twelve, I was already a few inches taller than the charismatic, though diminutive, evangelist.

A few months before Bishop Reilly died, I asked my father if we could go to Europe for the 100th anniversary of the Lourdes apparitions. I had seen *The Song of Bernadette* many times and wanted to see the locations for myself. Dad agreed, giving me many perks since I was an only child without a mother, and booked an entire "Catholic Pilgrimage" of Europe which included all the great shrines of London, Paris, Brussels and Rome.

We took off from Idlewild Airport (now JFK) on a shaky, propeller driven DC-7 Sabena Belgian Airlines plane that looked like the last effort of the Wright Brothers. Our first stop was Gander Newfoundland then on to Ireland, the greenest country in the world. We made stops in Killarney, Limerick and Dublin then on to London where we stayed at the very pish-posh Savoy. As we were leaving for a tour from the back entrance of the hotel, people were applauding a small man in a military uniform. It was Field Marshal Bernard Montgomery, an iconic hero of World War II.

The main attraction of the trip was a three day visit to the Brussels World's Fair. Our first stop was Shannon, Ireland where I stopped the immigration process cold by stating my profession was "altar boy". There were two priest-chaplains named Hewitt who were real-life brothers from Tom's River, New Jersey. They also saw me as a future priest and bought me a black priest's biretta which I wore all through the entire trip.

In Lourdes, I expected to see a full-blown miracle only to witness a sick man fall out of his wheelchair and crack his head on the cement. The viewing of the mummified body of St. Bernadette proved more creepy than inspiring and the home in which she lived was far more upscale than the dank prison portrayed in the film.

In Lourdes, I got one of the biggest unintentional laughs of my life and managed to mortify my father at the same time. There was just a sink and a bidet in our less than four star accommodations. I had no idea what that strange piece of plumbing was and my father was too embarrassed to tell me its actual purpose. He told me it was a footbath. The next morning when our group met in the lobby, one of the ladies was bemoaning the fact that she had to leave her room to use the bathroom. I chimed in, "You didn't have to. We just peed in the footbath!" Even the two chaplains were holding their sides laughing.

    The pinnacle of the trip came in Rome where we attended an audience of Pope Pius XII's and I stood close enough to almost touch him. The presence of this living saint was marred when he opened his mouth to bless the crowd and he sounded like Gracie Allen with a bad Italian accent.

    When we got to Paris, we visited every church in the city and met a Bishop John J. Boardman from Brooklyn, who as fate would have it, would become my pastor after the death of Bishop Reilly a few months later. Boardman was a ruddy-faced politician who could have been cast as a Senator as much as a prelate.

When he did become our pastor, my father reintroduced himself and reminded the Bishop that we had met and spent time with him in Paris only a few months before. Boardman, ever the glad-hander said, "Of course I remember you. I remember you very well. And how's your lovely wife?" "Dead," answered my father, "for ten years."

Although I was enjoying all the Saints and cathedrals my father was in search of a little more adult entertainment. Our tour guide suggested that he knew a little tourist-free strip club not far from the hotel. Dad decided that this was as good a way as any to teach me the difference between the sexes and so the three of us headed off.

The place was called Le Club Sexy, down a flight of stairs, and as cheesy a place as you could imagine. Right out of a movie. Smoke filled. Rowdy. Since Tony our Tour Guide knew the owners, we were escorted to a table right down front. As we entered, an overly voluptuous redhead was beginning her act as a cowgirl complete with two pistols shooting caps. After a sexy strip to a down-and-dirty version of "Don't Fence Me In," she brought out a saddle and demonstrated what trick riding was all about. I even felt a little tumescence.

As I entered the seventh grade it was all but decided that I would enroll in the minor seminary after graduation and take the first steps on my sacred path to be the first Brooklyn-born pope. And then my grandfather bought me a record player and that path was forever detoured. Pa, my mother's father, had bought the record player because I told everyone who would listen that I had sent away for a record album of Pope Pius XII singing Gregorian chant, but had nothing to play it on. The record player arrived before the pope's LP and so I went to the record store and picked up the first album I saw in the rack -- Ethel Merman in *Annie Get Your Gun*. I raced home to test the sound of my new phonograph and heard my first overture. Then came the voice of Merman. Oh that voice. Oh my God, that voice. She sang "Doing What Comes Naturally." Before I got to the next track, I replaced the needle and played it again. And again. Within a half hour I knew every word. My grandmother who lived with me, who we called Nana, was going out of her mind. Finally she came into the bedroom I shared with her and said, "Turn that screech owl off!" "Don't you like her?" I wanted to know. "No, she's a loudmouth multi-divorcee," came the reply. I didn't know why my Nana had linked her singing power to her marriages and didn't care about the connection. All I knew was that the voice inhabited every fiber of my body and perhaps had taken over my soul. After my grandmother went to sleep, I took the record player out to the living room and listened to the album all over again with my ear pressed against the speaker, the volume almost inaudible. My father came home with a half snootful, as usual, and asked me what I was listening to. Thinking it was permission, I turned the volume up full and Merman's voice inhabited the room. Dad started singing along with her to "There's no Business Like Show Business" and then said, "What a great show!"

"You saw her?"

"Saw her? I know her."

"What do you mean you know her?"

"Her dad is the CPA for my company. Ed Zimmermann. He's one of my best friends."

"Did you ever meet her?"

"Of course I've met her. I see her all the time when she comes down to have lunch with Ed. I've even taken her out to dinner a few times."

"Will she be my new mother?" I wanted to know.

"I don't think so," he said. "She's married to the head of Continental Airlines. We're not in the same league."

"What does that mean, daddy?"

"It means I couldn't afford her."

"Nana hates her voice." I offered.

"Well, she should hear her sing in person."

"I want to hear her sing in person," I said, almost jumping up and down. "Where does she sing?"

"She sings on Broadway. She's in Gypsy."

For a moment, "in Gypsy" sounded like one word and very Latin - like the pope making a pronouncement "Ingipsie."

"Can we go see it?" I begged.

"I don't think you're old enough."

I reminded him that our visit to Le Club Sexy in Paris took place when I was eleven.

The noise had awakened my grandmother who stood in the hall just in time to hear me say, "But you took me to see naked women when we went to Paris last year." My Uncle John, the original couch potato, was suddenly interested.

Nana choked, "Naked women?! What are you talking about? What naked women? What is he talking about, Pierre?"

Though my father was named Peter, Nana thought Pierre was a better first name to go with our French Canadian surname. My father had learned to defend himself all through grammar and high school every time one of the toughs yelled "Hey, pee-in-the-ear" and dad almost killed my grandmother when he went to get his working papers and saw on his birth certificate that he had been christened Peter, not Pierre.

"It was a harmless little nightclub," my father tried to explain.

"With naked women? Jimmy, go to bed. Your father and I need to have a good talk."

I did as I was told and from the bedroom I could hear the argument continue.

Outside in the living room, dad was trying to be respectful of his mother. He tried to explain that we had gotten there by accident because the joint was next to a church. I guess he didn't see the huge neon sign that kept flashing on and off reading, "Le Club Sexy." After a few minutes more, I heard him say to her, "Oh, be quiet and go to bed." Nana came in seconds later. I pretended to snore so that the conversation wouldn't continue and I wouldn't have to answer any questions.

I called my father at his office the next day and told him he had promised me to take me to see *Gypsy*. I knew he wouldn't remember. I had often used that trick to get what I wanted -- knowing dad would never remember because he was sloshed the night before. "Okay, I'll call Ed and get Ethel's house seats for the Saturday matinee, June 20th at 2:30 p.m.

Dad invited my grandmother and Uncle John to go with us, but she invoked the Legion of Decency which had condemned the musical as being too prurient for any Catholic of any age to see. She would not go and she would not permit her youngest child to go, even though he was 36 years old.

My father gave the other tickets away to two actor friends of his, Matt Tobin and Otto "Babe" Lohmann. Ed Zimmermann, Ethel's father, met us in front of the Broadway Theatre on West 53rd Street and handed us the tickets -- Ethel Merman's own house seats, E 101-104. I sat on the aisle.

I had actually seen one other Broadway show -- a straight play -- when I was 11, due to my love of science fiction. I was home sick from school one day when I watched an afternoon interview show featuring an appearance by Cyril Ritchard. Ritchard had played Captain Hook brilliantly in the Broadway and television presentations of *Peter Pan* opposite Mary Martin, but now he was promoting a show called *A Visit To A Small Planet* by Gore Vidal. I loved anything that had to do with space travel and so when my father came home, I asked him to take me to see it. He didn't make the connection with science fiction, only proud that his eleven-year-old son wanted to see a Gore Vidal play. The show was at the Booth Theatre and I did not expect the lights to go down and to be in the dark before the curtain went up. I expected a planetarium show, but when the curtain rose, we were in a suburban living room with very earthly characters whose every other word was "bastard" or "son of a bitch." My grandmother, sitting next to me, flinched every time an epithet was uttered. The whole experience enchanted me but didn't prepare me for the transforming and life changing experience that was Ethel Merman in *Gypsy*.

As we took our seats in the fifth row and listened as the orchestra tuned , there was a buzz of excitement that filled the theatre. It was like church but with energy. The overture began, the trumpets blared, the curtain went up and Ethel Merman swept down the aisle right next to me shouting, "Sing out, Louise! Smile, baby!"

By the time two hours had passed, I experienced a religious conversion the likes of which I had never felt in Lourdes or Rome. *Visit To A Small Planet* had been a three act play and I was shattered that the Gypsy cast started taking its bows after only two acts. I didn't want it to be over. It had to go on forever. And even though the show had been condemned by the Legion of Decency for some inexplicable reason, the girls in the burlesque scenes still wore scads more than those at Le Club Sexy.

When the house lights came on, my shaky legs barely got me out of my seat and carried me around the corner to the stage door where we were going to meet Mr. Zimmermann. He would then take us through to the backstage to meet his daughter. The doorman told us that Miss Merman was on the stage -- waiting for us. We could go right out. It was like walking onto holy ground.

She was still in the same lavender dress she wore for *Rose's Turn*, the electrifying finale of the show.

"Hiya, pop!" said Ethel as she greeted her dad. "Hiya, Pete," she said as she gave my dad a kiss on the cheek. "And this must be Jimmy."

Oh my God, she knew my name. I could feel the stagehands swirling around us putting the sets in order for the evening show but I could not take my eyes off of Merman. My first thought was that she was taller than Bishop Sheen.

She must have thought me to be an idiot because I couldn't answer any of her questions. "Did you like the show?" "How were the seats?" "Have you seen a Broadway show before?" "What grade are you in?" And then, the curtain of the Broadway Theatre went up and I looked out into the house with its rows of blue and gold seats and huge windows on either side of the stage.

Then came the question from Merman, "So what do you want to be when you grow up?" I always had a ready answer to that question which I had been asked hundreds of times, "I'm going to be a priest." But this time, I had no answer except to stare into the empty Broadway Theatre and mumble, "This!"

Seeing *Gypsy* and meeting Merman was a greater religious experience than receiving the communion wafer for the first time. I knew I wanted to be onstage more than anything in the world and so like Mickey and Judy I decided to put on a show.

I was lucky that I lived in a huge apartment complex with many amenities. Flagg Court was built in the Beaux Arts style in 1933 by Ernest Flagg, architect of the Singer Building in New York. The seven "units" filled an entire Bay Ridge block surrounding an Olympic sized swimming pool, bowling alleys, tennis and handball courts. But what I was most interested in was the three hundred seat auditorium.

I made an appointment to go to see the manager of the theater who was expecting some older man who could pay full price for a rental. Jack Rubak was quite surprised when ten neighborhood kids, led by me, told him we wanted to put on a revue and raise money for the Cancer Society. He was so taken with the idea that he gave us the theatre and would supply the concessions for free.

So I wrote, directed and of course starred in *The Flagg Court Follies of 1959*. I sang a head-scratching version of "Bali Hai" and closed the first act with an unforgettable rendition of "Give My Regards To Broadway" backed by eight leggy twelve year old girls. Our adventure made the local papers and the place was packed. We raised $300 for the Cancer Society and my father told me he thought I was a natural talent and was very proud of what I had done. The only person wasn't happy about the show was my grandmother Minnie who saw that my road to the priesthood had just taken a detour. The course of my life was forever changed the day I saw *Gypsy*.. The road to Rome became the road to Broadway and worship of the Virgin Mary was transferred to the great Merm.

I ended up seeing *Gypsy* a dozen times over the almost two years it played on Broadway and saw Merman every time after. She always greeted me warmly. Always had time. A few years later, we had dinner with Ethel and her parents, Ed and Agnes, at Toots Shor's Restaurant on West 52nd Street.

It was a sad dinner because Ed was going blind and Ethel had to cut his meat for him and help move his food around the plate to find the pieces. Ed started crying, not wanting to be a burden to his family. He couldn't work anymore because he couldn't see the numbers in front of him -- rendering him useless as a CPA. This realization seemed to hit at dinner with his daughter cutting his meat for him and little Agnes holding back the tears watching.

I told my friend Stan Freeman who had conducted for Ethel often about the incident. "Getting old isn't pretty," he said. "If I ever get to that point, I think I'll just end it all." In January of 2001, he did just that.

Stan Freeman was my best friend for thirty years and I learned that one of the reasons Stanley was not a well-known name except for show business circles was that he did too many things too well. I believe Stan was one of the greatest piano players of the 20th Century. His most famous gig was playing the harpsichord on the Rosie Clooney recording of "Come On A My House."

He composed two Broadway shows. The first was *I Had A Ball* in 1964 with Buddy Hackett, which was a moderate success and in 1970, *Lovely Ladies, Kind Gentlemen* which was one of the best-known flops in the history of Broadway.

Clive Barnes review of the show caused the cast to picket him and the New York Times when he wrote a scathing assessment of the musical beginning with "I come not to praise *Lovely Ladies*, but to bury it!" And he did. The show which starred Ken Nelson, Ron Hussmann and David Burns, closed after limping along for two weeks.

The ironic thing about *Lovely Ladies* is that it wasn't a bad show. Those who saw the show enjoyed it very much. It was not the greatest musical ever, but certainly not worthy of Barnes's scorn. It was the wrong show for the wrong time. Nobody wanted to see the musical version of *Teahouse of the August Moon*, about soldiers occupying the Japanese island of Okinawa, while the Vietnam was raging on. All-Singing, All-Dancing Asians (played by whites) wasn't what the Broadway audiences were craving in 1971. But I saw almost every one of the sixteen performances because one of the stars of the show was my mentor and pal, David Burns. I had always been looking for another mother, but in David Burns, I found another father. And then came Crawford.

CHAPTER TWO
Latitudes and Attitudes

With Joan, her daughters Cathy and Cindy and my dad.

July 1, 1960 - En Route to Rio De Janeiro

Just as our Bon Voyage party on the *S.S. Brasil* was peaking, dad's drinking buddy, Bill King, came lurching into the cabin to announce that Joan Crawford had booked space somewhere on the ship and was sailing with us. I had no idea who Joan Crawford was but everyone in the room was thrilled about it. Mr. King, who was absolutely bombed, suggested we go to Crawford's stateroom and introduce ourselves. I was trying to keep an eye on my grandfather, Dick Condon, who was also on his way to total oblivion since he wouldn't relinquish his seat in our cabin and the other partygoers kept pouring scotch down his throat.

Dad told me Joan Crawford was one of the greatest movie stars of all time -- an Oscar winner -- and suddenly I was interested. We formed a small welcome aboard committee, went down to the public room where Miss Crawford's bon voyage party was in full swing.

I only got a glimpse of her back. Her head was covered in an enormous black picture hat. Bill King stepped in front of me and slobbered, "Miss Crawford, may I kiss you?" Without seeing the reaction on her face, all I heard was a soft, sweet "No."

One of the saddest things about the takeover of the terrorists these days is the demise of the bon voyage party on the great ships. Back in the sixties, anyone was welcomed aboard to celebrate the departure of their friends on an ocean voyage. For a fifty-cent contribution to the Norwegian Seamen's Fund, the ship was open to all visitors. Dad decided that we would go on a cruise the summer before I was shipped off to Military school.

The *S.S. Brasil* was the flagship of the Moore-McCormack Lines which was half freighter and half luxury passenger ship that made monthly voyages between New York and Buenos Aires with stops in Barbados, Caracas, Trinidad, Sao Paulo, Rio de Janeiro and Montevideo. Joan was not the only celebrity aboard. The great theatrical caricaturist Al Hirschfeld was also sailing with his wife, Dolly, and daughter, Nina, who he immortalized by placing her name in all of his artwork. But Joan Crawford was the only person my father wanted to know. And he did. Biblically.

The announcement blasted through the stateroom, "All ashore that's going ashore." My grandfather tried to stand but couldn't. The fourteen scotches he poured down during the soiree had robbed him of his power of locomotion.

My mother's father was a fascinating man who started out as a fireman in New York City when horses drew the trucks through the streets. He won the James Gordon Bennett Medal for heroism, the highest honor the Department could bestow on any of its firemen because he saved ten lives during the infamous Triangle Shirt Factory Fire in 1911. But as we were preparing to sail, he was sloshed and incapable of movement. We propped him up against the door of the stateroom and told him to stand there as we found his hat and coat. When we turned around, he was gone.

We panicked because the ship was about to sail and Pa (as we called him) was gone. Not in the passageway. Not in the elevators. Not on the decks. Vanished. Dad was about to make arrangements for him to go all the way to Rio with us. The Promenade Deck was lined with partying passengers, throwing streamers and confetti to their friends on the shore. We looked down the pier to see if we spotted Pa but he was nowhere to be seen. Then, as I looked down to an opening in the hull on the lower part of the ship where there was a conveyor belt bringing food on. It suddenly stopped and began rotating the other way toward the dock. Pa appeared on the conveyor belt supported by two crew members holding him under both arms and was rolled off to shore.

The *Brasil* pulled out into New York harbor and began slowly sailing down the Hudson into the Narrows and passed the apartment house in which we lived. We didn't sail under the Verrazano Narrows Bridge because it had not yet been built. I felt so lucky to live right on the Bay and I loved great ocean liners more than anything in the world. I would run to the roof early in the morning to see the new ships sail into the harbor on their inaugural call to New York, greeted by the fire boats spraying them with a rainbow-infused welcome.

I even watched the *Stockholm* limp into the harbor the day after it rammed the side of the *Andrea Doria* and sank it. The sight of the ship with its bow seared off was chilling, especially after watching the footage of the great Italian liner sink the night before.

The first day at sea on the *Brasil* there was a mixer for all the teenagers on board so I went and met twin girls named Cindy and Cathy who were exactly my age. The cruise director, Danny Leone, hosted the party which lasted a few hours and made sure we knew the names of all the others kids our age on board. When the party was over, Cindy and Cathy invited me back to their cabin to play board games and I accepted. They wanted me to meet their mother, who was recently widowed. Always on the lookout for a new mother, I thought, "Why not?"

When we came into the cabin, their mother was sitting at the vanity table dying her hair. She greeted us all with a smile and welcomed a game of Scrabble on the stateroom floor. Within an hour, I knew I had found my perfect stepmother along with two built-in stepsisters. My father didn't want any part of it.

"But daddy, she's really beautiful!"

"I know a lot of beautiful women," he snarled.

"And she's a widow."

"I don't want to meet any widows," he confirmed. "And I don't want to get married again. I'm not getting married again. So don't do any matchmaking because you're just wasting your time."

Back in the sixties, every night aboard a ship was a formal night with the ladies in elegant gowns and the men in tuxes. I always thought the guys had it easy because the tux was like a uniform -- you didn't have to decide what to wear -- a tux was a tux -- unless you had a white dinner jacket and then you had to decide.

Dad dressed early and looked like a movie star in his formal clothes. He went to the Captain's "Welcome Aboard" cocktail party early in hope that his favorite movie star would show up and he could wrangle an invitation for a dance. Alas, she was a no-show. I still hadn't made the connection that Cindy and Cathy's mom, with whom I had spent the afternoon, was Joan Crawford. When the waiter came in to deliver her ice bucket he only addressed her as "Mrs. Steele."

Our table in the dining room of the *Brasil* was all the way at the back, a table for two against the wall. Just after dad had ordered his cocktail and I was pondering a double order of mashed potatoes; a smattering of applause began to sound at the entrance to the room. The applause grew to a roar and then a standing ovation. Dad saw her at a distance and almost spit out his Chivas Regal.

"There she is," he said. "Omigod. There she is. Isn't she beautiful? God, she looks great. Should I go say hello. No. I'll meet her sometime."

Although her table was next to the Captain's, she kept coming right toward us. Dad looked behind him to see who she was looking at only to come face to face with the wall. When he turned back, she was standing right in front of us, beaming, Cindy and Cathy demurely and properly behind her.

"Jimmy, dear!" she started. "Don't you look handsome in your dinner jacket? Thank you so much for spending the afternoon with us. What a good Scrabble player you are." I looked at dad whose jaw was lying on the salad plate.

"And this must be Pete," she continued. "I've been hearing a lot about you. Since you work on Wall Street,

I'm sure we have many friends in common -- and we have a whole month together to find out. Shall we have a cocktail after dinner…and a dance perhaps?"

If you were to open a dictionary at that moment and look up the word *speechless*, you would find a picture of my father. He could barely utter a sound as he shook her outstretched hand and nodded. The girls also put their white gloved hands out but my father never took his eyes off Joan as he shook them. Even though I was only 13, I could not help but notice that there was a spark between the two of them. Joan looked back over her shoulder as the maitre'd led them to their own table and she gave dad a wink which had the effect of having his legs pulled out from under him.

Knowing Joan was experiencing my first taste of what it was like to be a star. On the cruise down the East Coast of South America, we made stops at Sao Paulo, Rio De Janeiro, Montevideo and Buenos Aires, and at every port the piers were jammed with local residents trying to get just a glimpse of the great Crawford. The turnout was massive. Joan was there on Pepsi business and scheduled a press conference for every stop.

I couldn't imagine how many steamer trunks she had brought since there was a new outfit for every city, a different dress for every day and she never wore the same evening gown twice in thirty days. On the third night of the trip, my father did not come back to the cabin until morning. He woke me up at seven a.m. trying not to wake me up. I told him I was worried and went looking for him about three a.m. He told me he was spending time with a new friend.

A few hours later, I ran into Cindy and Cathy. They couldn't help me since their mother had a private bedroom in the suite. Dad didn't show up for several nights, and years later -- after they stopped seeing each other and I was old enough to understand -- he admitted to a torrid affair that lasted years after the ship returned to port.

After *Whatever Happened To Baby Jane?* was released, I went to see the film with my best buddy from grammar school, Joey Maresca. I kept telling Joey that the woman who played Blanche was my friend and though he knew I had met her on the *Brasil* several years before, refused to believe that she was indeed my "friend." Joan lived at 2 East 70th Street at the corner of Fifth Avenue which wasn't far from where we had seen the film.

"If you know her so well," he challenged, "let's go visit her."

"Okay," said I, "Let's go."

It was the middle of our Easter vacation and we were dressed, as my grandmother would say, like ragamuffins. We got to the apartment door where the doorman looked down his nose at us and silently implied to just keep walking. Instead, we went up to him and I said, "We'd like to see Mrs. Steele please."

"She's not home," he barked.

"She's expecting us," I lied. "And if she's not home, Cindy and Cathy will be."

He looked at us quizzically, cocking his head to the side somewhat like a beagle that had heard a high frequency sound, and went inside. We could see him on the phone as he looked back and forth before returning with a somewhat smile drooping under his nose.

"She said you could go right up."

Joey looked as astonished as the doorman as we were escorted -- not to the main elevator -- but to the service elevator in the rear of the lobby.

Joan's faithful German housekeeper, affectionately known as Mamacita was standing in the kitchen as the elevator door opened onto the small service hallway.

"Jeeeemy!" she bellowed, enveloping me in her endless arms, "Missus is waiting for you. And the girls are here!" Then she added, "You know what to do!" Indeed I did. Before you could enter Joan's apartment, you had to take off your shoes to prevent any outside dirt from creeping onto her pure white carpets. Things got off to a rocky start when Joey protested. I told him that was as far as he went if he didn't. I couldn't blame him. He shed his shoes to reveal a huge hole with his big right toe sticking through it.

Mamacita escorted us through the immaculate white living room into the den/office where Joan stood behind her desk, framed by a large picture window overlooking Fifth Avenue and Central Park. Cindy and Cathy sat on couches on either side of the room, giving the impression that the scene had been staged. The girls were in matching pink sundresses and Joan was put together as though the director was about to shout, "Action!"

Joan came around the desk and kissed me on each cheek. Cindy and Cathy followed suit. Joey was dumbstruck. The person we had just seen in *Baby Jane* was standing in front of him live and in person. Joan couldn't have more gracious or welcoming, despite the fact that we were there uninvited.

"Thank you so much for stopping by. The girls are home for Easter and you were so kind to think of us."

"Joan," I started. "This is Joey Maresca. We just saw *Whatever Happened to Baby Jane?*"

"I hope you enjoyed it," she smiled.

"It was great," we both stammered.

"Can I offer you something to drink?"

Joey answered first. It was an answer that sent chills down my spine.

"I'll have a Coke," he said.

The girls' eyes widened and they both looked at their Pepsi-wielding mother for guidance. Joan's smile was implacable.

"I'm so sorry, Joseph" she offered. "We don't serve Coke here. Wouldn't you like a Pepsi?"

Joey winced. "No, I don't like Pepsi!"

Cathy actually gasped audibly but Joan continued to smile. "You don't?"

"No," he said, "It's too sweet!"

Still smiling, albeit now a frozen smile, she offered a glass of water.

The affair Joan had with my dad lasted about a year but my friendship with Joan endured until she died.

From the very first time I met Joan, she was on me that I was way too fat and had to lose weight. This was to be an ongoing struggle lasting for years -- within myself and with Joan. Almost every letter I (or my father) got from her over the years addressed the "problem." For example:

August 19, 1964

Pete darling,

I am distressed with the news about Jimmy's weight - my God, fifty pounds. He must get on a diet. Send him to Dr. Jerome Klein at 1 East 69th Street, will you?

He was very helpful with Cindy who weighs 164 now and should weigh 124. But Cindy has refused to work with the doctor and he has refused to work with her until she gets down to at least 155.

Herbert Barnet's niece went to Dr. Klein and she has trimmed herself down into the most beautiful young lady you ever saw. Have Jimmy checked thoroughly before you send him, naturally, but it would be a good idea. It would give him something to do and a responsibility of his own.

Love,
Joan

In 1966, when I was 20 years old, I wrote to Joan seeking guidance about what to do with the rest of my life. My father wanted me to study law and follow in his footsteps on Wall Street, but I had fallen in love with show business and was very influenced by Davy Burns. I wrote to Joan and, even in trying to give me advice about my career path, she still managed to pick on me for being overweight.

March 10, 1966
Jimmy dear,
How nice it was to receive your newsy letter. It's interesting that you've done so many things in such a short time, but I think now, at twenty, you had better settle down into something you're really going to do. You know that I am your friend at all times, but I must tell you that even though you are six feet four, 200 pounds is too much weight for you. But I am extremely proud that you lost 55 pounds.

You mentioned that you are trying to do what your father wants you to do. You've always been very close to him.

I think he's right and I think that Davy Burns is right - show business is rough. There are very few who make it like Davy Burns. It takes discipline beyond belief and work, work, work. Of course the other jobs you've been seeking take discipline too, but not nearly as much as acting.

The other jobs you've been seeking require perhaps more knowledge college-wise. Acting requires knowledge of people and understanding of people.

I am going off on a business trip for Pepsi-Cola tomorrow, but will be back in New York around March 20th. If you would like to come up and have a talk with me, I would be delighted to see you again.

Or you may surely call me on the telephone. My number is still Murray Hill 8-4500. Bless you and have a nice talk with your father, okay? And I am always here if you need me.
Love,
Joan

April 5, 1967
Jimmy dear,
Loved your letter but am so sad to hear that your weight is still a problem. Do take care and my love to you and your father.
Joan

February 13, 1968
Jimmy dear,
How wonderful you have lost all that weight! I'm so proud of you. As you said, after getting over the first big hurdle, the rest should be a breeze. Stay with it now. God bless and my love to you and your dad.
Joan

November 29, 1968

Jimmy dear,
I'm delighted you're maintaining a B average at school but do push a little for some A's! It's too bad about your weight. Be a good lad and push away from the table while you're still hungry, Jimmy dear - that's the secret of dieting. And no between meal eating of any kind and no bread, butter, potatoes or deserts (sic).
All love, Joan

JOAN CRAWFORD

March 10, 1966

Jimmy dear,

How nice it was to receive your newsy letter. It's interesting that you've done so many things in such a short time, but I think now, at twenty, you had better settle down into something you're really going to do. You know that I am your friend at all times, but I must tell you that even though you are six feet four, 200 pounds is too much weight for you. But I am extremely proud that you lost 55 pounds.

You mentioned that you are trying to do what your father wants you to do. You've always been very close to him. I think he's right and I think that Davy Burns is right - show business is rough. There are very few who make it like Davy Burns. It takes discipline beyond belief and work, work, work. Of course the other jobs you've been seeking take discipline too, but not nearly as much as acting. The other jobs you've been seeking require perhaps more knowledge college-wise. Acting requires knowledge of people and understanding of people.

I am going off on a business trip for Pepsi-Cola tomorrow, but will be back in New York around March 20th. If you would like to come up and have a talk with me, I would be delighted to see you again. Or you may surely call me on the telephone. My number is still Murray Hill 8-4500.

Bless you and have a nice talk with your father, okay? And I am always here if you need me.

love
Joan

I took Joan up on her offer, called her and made a date to go to the apartment and spend an evening with her. When I got to 2 East 70th St. the doorman announced me and I went up – this time through the front elevator. The elevator doors opened right into the apartment and I was greeted by a short lady in a pink house coat, her hair covered with a matching scarf and no makeup. I said, "Hi. I'm Jimmy and I'm here to see Joan." The little lady said, "Who the hell do you think I am? I don't look that bad, do I?"

Of course I wanted to get right back in the elevator and die. I had just never seen Joan since that first day so many years ago without makeup and a perfectly coiffed hairdo. She chuckled, reminded me to take off my shoes and led me into the kitchen where she was making bouillabaisse for a dinner party the next night -- chain smoking and sipping vodka. She was a little tipsy, offered me the mandatory Pepsi and I sat on a stool at the kitchen counter talking while she cooked.

She was very interested in why I wanted to be an actor and why I thought I could be a success at it. I told her about the passion I had for the theatre and thought I was pretty good in all the plays I had done. She said, "Well the odds are very much against you." Once again she harped about my weight and said that I was too tall to make movies. I couldn't see how that made a difference. I told her I was really a stage actor. She asked me if I was disciplined? I told her I didn't think so. She put down her big spoon, looked at me and said, "Jimmy! Discipline, discipline, discipline! If you have it you can make it; if you don't you won't. You must do something for your career every day. Even if it's only a phone call."

We talked about work ethics and such and she emphasized that once she knew what she wanted she put her heart and soul into it. Then out of the blue she said, "I always knew I'd be a star as long as my back held out."

Now I must admit I was very naive and wasn't quite sure what she was referring to. I thought she meant that hard work was going to break her back. About two years later, all of a sudden, I had an epiphany of what she was actually talking about. There was no secret that Joan was a very highly sexual person. At least my father thought so. She had a horrific childhood, suffering abuse of every imaginable kind at the hands of her stepfather. It's no wonder she was a little fucked up. Anybody who went through that kind of trauma would be. But she pulled herself up and became one of the most famous women in the world. That's what I call discipline. The television was on in the background and a pizza commercial came on.

"What fun it would be to just go out for a pizza." she sighed.

"Come on, " I said. "Let's go for a pizza!"

"I can't. It would take me an hour to get ready."

I remember I looked at her not understanding because she continued, "Don't you know I can't leave this house unless I'm Joan Crawford -- and besides, you don't need a pizza."

Years later, I became very close with Lucille Ball, who was just the opposite. If the urge for a pizza came over her, she would throw on some lipstick and out the door we'd go.

Sadly, Joan's reputation is tainted by the evil that her daughter perpetrated after her death. Christina was a talentless and jealous girl who decided to make a reputation by trashing her mother. Shame on her. Her other two daughters, Cindy and Cathy, would absolutely dispute all the things that Christina said.

Betty Barker, her decades-long secretary, told me that she witnessed Christina's "bad seed" behavior. Christina knew why Joan hated wire hangers. It was one of the reminders of her horrible childhood. You see Joan had to put herself through St. Agnes Academy by working in the school's hot, airless laundry. Joan's job? Iron the rich girls' blouses and put them on wire hangers. Betty Barker said when Joan got home from the studio she was too exhausted to take an axe to shrubs or slap the kids around. Betty said those things just didn't happen.

While Joan was concerned about my dieting, she had the kind of fast metabolism that precluded her from gaining even an ounce. Mine was and is still slower than Lincoln Tunnel traffic at rush hour. In the course of my life I have gained and lost the weight of the Taj Mahal.
Joan gave me so much of herself in the seventeen years we were friends and she also gave me one of the greatest memories of my life -- meeting President John F. Kennedy.

In late October 1963, Joan called and asked my father to escort her to an affair at the New York Hilton where the President was to receive an award as father of the year from the Protestant Council of America. I would be home from military school and was also invited to go. The grand ballroom of the Hilton was packed and in the next room was a dinner for the Catholic Actors Guild presided over by actor Horace MacMahon and filmdom's "Blondie," Penny Singleton.

What surprised me most about the evening was the lack of security. Our table was in the back while Joan sat on the dais near the president. People from all parts of the hotel just ambled in to get a glimpse of Kennedy and no one stopped them. I even walked from the back of the hall down to the stage to get a closer look and not one secret service agent or security guard tried to keep me from him.

I stood at the side of the ballroom -- no more than fifty feet away from him -- and was awed by the presence of the man. He was not only dynamic but incredibly handsome and charismatic. What I will never forget was the redness of his hair -- bright, almost carrot red -- a shade that never showed up in any color picture I ever saw of him.

Joan saw me standing to the side and when the president finished his speech to wild applause, she nodded for me to come closer to the edge of the dais where he was about to exit. Kennedy shook hands with everyone along the head table as he made his way out and I managed to get to the side where he was about to step off. Joan was next to him and waved for me to come forward. Still, no one tried to stop me. Kennedy was right next to me now, taller than I expected and Joan was next to him. He was about to go out the door when she said, "Mr. President, I'd like to introduce you to my friend, James Brochu."

"How do you do, James." said Kennedy as I shook his hand. "You're a big lad. Do you play football?"

"No, sir," I answered, "I'm on the speech and debate team." "Well, that's fine," he continued as he kept moving and was out the door. Two weeks later he was shot dead.

At another dinner, a year earlier, held at the old Commodore Hotel on 42nd Street (now the Grand Hyatt), Joan introduced me to another icon, Eleanor Roosevelt. Mrs. Roosevelt was giving a speech about the UN and presenting an award to Bob Hope. I actually worked with Mr. Hope ten years later and found him to be a completely nasty and horrible person -- but more on that sad tale later.

I was wearing my high school uniform, a knock-off of the cadet grays used by the United States Military Academy. Mrs. Roosevelt was very short and hunched over. Looking up at me with a cocked head, she saw my uniform and asked if I went to West Point? "No, Mrs. Roosevelt," I said. "I go to La Salle Military Academy on Long Island."

"Who are your teachers?" she continued.

"The Christian Brothers of St. La Salle," I answered proudly.

"Oh," she said with obvious disappointment. "Papist!"

The last time I talked to Joan was Easter, 1976. It was the first and only time she had called just to chat. It was late at night and I could tell that she had been drinking. She kept calling me by my father's name, "Pete." I would say, "This is Jimmy, Joan." "Ah yes, Pete. How is Jimmy? Nice boy. Too fat."

I kept in the touch with Joan receiving long, newsy letters from time to time. The last note I got from her was a handwritten birthday greeting, not the usual typed letter with a signature and note. On May 10, 1977 I was riding in the back of a cab going north on Market Street in San Francisco. I looked out the window and saw a newspaper hawker holding up the evening edition of *The Chronicle*. The headline blared "Joan Crawford Dead."

It was the end of a friendship and the end of an era. My friend Ray Stricklyn was Bette Davis' publicist. He played her son in *The Catered Affair* and then went to work for super-publicist John Springer. Upon the news of Joan's demise he called Bette and said, "Bette, Joan Crawford died." Bette's response: "Eh! Just cause you die, it doesn't mean you change."

Oh, and there was another teenager I met that first day on the S.S. *Brasil*. Her name was Janet and we learned that she and her family lived only a few blocks from us in Bay Ridge. We became friends immediately and have stayed friends for over fifty years.

And she went from doing the Limbo with me to running the Federal Reserve for Barack Obama. Yes, Janet Yellen and I go that far back. I must have had a crush on her because I gave her my high school class ring. Steve and I had dinner with her not long ago and she told me she still had the ring and was keeping it. I told her it was okay; it didn't fit anymore anyway.

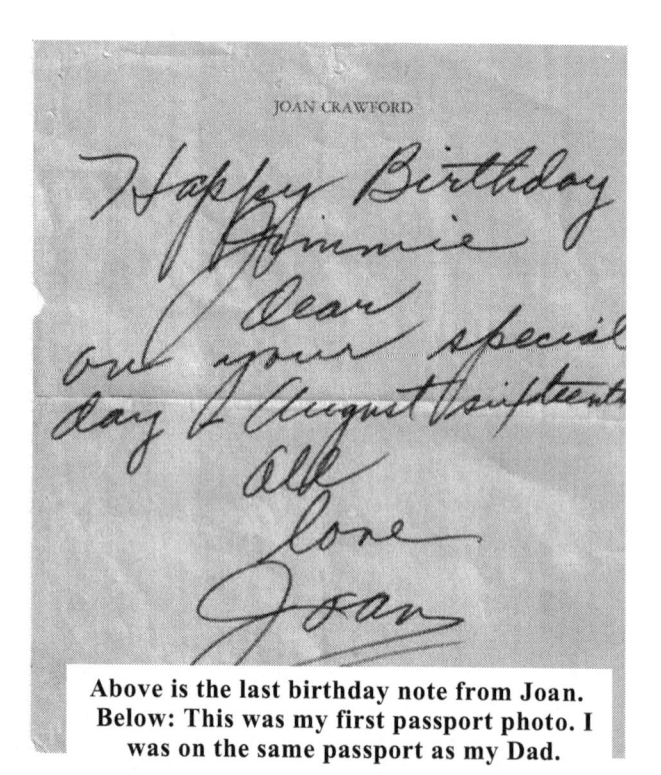

JOAN CRAWFORD

Happy Birthday Jimmie dear on your special day — August sixteenth. All love, Joan

Above is the last birthday note from Joan. Below: This was my first passport photo. I was on the same passport as my Dad.

Former Federal Reserve Chairman Janet Yellen and I wowing the other kids in a Limbo contest aboard the S.S. *Brasil* en route to South America. The crowd kept shouting, "How low can you go?" Years later people would be asking her the same question about interest rates. Below, the two of us just a few years later. She me she was keeping the ring

CHAPTER THREE
A Mentor and A. Miller

Davy Burns backstage at the 46th Street Theatre after *The Price*

One night, after seeing *A Funny Thing Happened on the Way to the Forum* at the Alvin Theatre next door to Jilly's, I walked in to find dad with a microphone in his hand singing a duet of "Hey, Jealous Lover" with JUDY GARLAND! They were both bombed but having a wonderful time. Dad brought Judy over and introduced us as if they were old friends, but they had only met an hour before over a bottle of Johnnie Walker Red. I guess alcoholics bond quickly. In a strange way I found it very fitting that when dad died in November of 1984, he died on a Friday night at exactly 8:15 pm. His night to howl.

I was alone at home in Brooklyn on another Friday - March 12, 1971 when the phone rang at 11 p.m. and it was actress Mary Jo Catlett who called to tell me that my best friend and mentor had just died of a heart attack. His name was David Burns. He died on the stage of the Forrest Theatre in Philadelphia during the tryout of the Kander and Ebb musical, *70 Girls, 70*.

I called him my Uncle even though he was not a blood relative. It just seemed the easiest way to explain the relationship since we were fairly inseparable. I was a young teenager when I first met him backstage at *Forum* when he was in his late fifties. He was my idol, my hero, my second father, my inspiration, my friend and as George Burns once told me, "the greatest comic actor that ever lived." He dazzled me with his personality, awed me with his talent, staggered me with his friendship and I wanted to be him when I grew up.

Davy Burns was the man I loved. It was purely platonic and absolutely unsexual. He was militantly heterosexual and took his sexual humor far over the edge for the 1950s and 60s. To say he was outrageous would be like calling Madonna a real virgin. Today he would be viewed as crass, vulgar and a borderline pervert. He wouldn't hesitate to back a chorus girl against a corner and tell her, "I'd love to fuck you!"

Academy Award winning actor Jack Albertson, who went on to wide fame in television as "the man" of *Chico and The Man* told me that gay men were also one of Davy's favorite "targets." Jack told me, "We went to Schrafft's one night for a soda while Dave was in *Dolly* and I was in *The Subject Was Roses*. All the waiters were a little "swishy" and they adored David. David ordered a pineapple soda and called the waiter over to whisper in his ear. The waiter bent down, and in his sweetest tone, Dave said, "I'd love to fuck you." The waiter replied in an equally loving tone, "It'll cost you." Davy said, "How much?" The waiter said, "Two tickets to *Hello, Dolly!*" David said, "For two tickets to *Dolly!,* you can fuck <u>me</u>."

Today it would be considered sexual harassment and a lawsuit, but then it was a slap on the hand and a giggle at the paper tiger. He was an adorable letch who could get away with murder from the power of his cuteness. He had a lust for Black hotel maids, smoked cheap cigars, wore unmatched clothes that he inherited from old shows and for the height of contradiction was a devout atheist married to a beautiful Christian Science Practitioner.

Jack Albertson also reminisced about the time he and Davy were appearing with Bert Lahr in the road company of *Make Mine Manhattan.* "After the show one night in Boston, we went over to the Town and Country nightclub where our old friend Mickey Alpert was singing. It was so crowded that particular night that they had to set up tables on the stage and we were all lit by the spill of the spotlights. A group of us from the show sat down and then Davy disappeared. A few minutes later, while Mickey was singing, Davy comes out of the kitchen wearing a woman's dress. Then a woman popped her head out of the kitchen and said, "I don't know who you are, but you better give me my dress back." The audience screamed, and poor Mickey didn't know what to do so he just kept on singing. But that was just the beginning.

Davy returned to the kitchen and came back out a few minutes later wearing his suit. He walked over to a ringside table, next to Mickey who is singing his heart out. Davy picked up some man's drink, took a gulp, spit it all over the stage and deposited the rest down the front of his pants. The audience howled. Davy did it again with a fresh drink and the laughs got even bigger. All of a sudden, Davy let loose and from anywhere on any table in sight, he opened his fly and started stuffing it with celery, olives, antipasto, salad, French fried potatoes, string beans, coleslaw and the audience was just on the floor. Mickey couldn't sing anymore because he was laughing too hard. Finally, the laughs started to die down, Davy reached for a breadstick, stuffed it into his open fly, looked at his crotch and screamed, 'It looks so good I think I'll eat it myself.'"

One of the legendary stories about Davy happened while he was playing Mayor Shinn in the original Broadway production of *The Music Man*, and he scandalized Robert Preston during a rehearsal break. Davy liked Preston very much but felt he was very strait-laced and just a bit too prissy.

Morton "Teak" DeCosta, the show's director, called a ten minute break and Davy followed Preston into the men's room, where he stood at the urinal next to him. As the two men relieved themselves, Davy stood back from the urinal and started to spray his pee from a long distance in an effort to get Preston's attention. When Robert Preston looked down at Davy's dick, he saw that it had a black ribbon tied around it.

Preston jumped back, spraying a stream of pee as he gasped at the sight.

"David! Is that a black ribbon around your...your...penis?"

Davy started to cry crocodile tears, weeping shamelessly as he said, "Yes, it is. Christian Dior died today in Paris and I'm in mourning."

One night after a performance of *A Funny Thing Happened on the Way to the Forum*, Davy backed up Myrna White, who was playing one of the courtesans, into the small elevator just inside the stage door of the Alvin Theatre.

It was an old elevator, probably the original that was installed when the theatre was built in 1923. It had a manually operated gate and a crank handle that would set the tiny car into operation.

Myrna got into the elevator, and before John Carradine and Jack Gilford could follow, Davy closed the gate and raised the elevator about two feet off the ground, providing an elevated stage for the waiting actors. Davy pushed Myrna against the wall and began kissing her on her shoulder, her arms, around her breasts, across her belly button and stopping short at her G-string.

Between Myra's screams and the cast's roars of approval, Davy stopped suddenly and waited for the hysteria to subside. He looked up at Myrna, who was enjoying it as much as everyone else. and in a voice that sounded like Bert Lahr's cowardly lion bellowed, "I'm sorry my dear, I can't go any further. I'm a vegetarian." With that, Myrna fell down laughing, Carradine and Gilford applauded, all the actors cheered and Davy pushed down on the crank that lifted the elevator out of sight.

My father's alcoholism had its benefits. One of those benefits was getting to know Davy Burns. In June of 1962, I got a ticket to see *A Funny Thing Happened on the Way to the Forum*. The cast included some of the most legendary actors in show business - John Carradine, Jack Gilford, Raymond Walburn - headed by the incarnation of theatrical insanity himself, Zero Mostel.

My father had an odd habit of showing up backstage at Broadway theatres after performances I would attend. I can only hazard that he got past the doormen by looking so distinguished that they thought he was a movie star but just couldn't place his name.

He had a chance to be a movie star once. A talent scout saw him and invited him to audition at the Paramount Studios in Astoria. He got to the studio on time but never went through the front gate. I asked him once why he didn't take the opportunity and he only said, "I didn't believe in myself."

I don't know if Davy Burns believed in himself. He had a remarkable career that started by accident in 1919 when he was 17 and saw a sign in his Chinatown High School that the Metropolitan Opera House needed "Spear Carriers" for one of their productions. The pay was two dollars a show. David was the breadwinner in his family because his father, a New York City cop named Nathan Bernstein, had been killed in the line of duty.

Davy's mother had no skills to support her three fatherless children - David, her oldest and his younger brother and sister, Joe and Tessie. The family needed to eat, Tessie needed to go to school and Joe had to have his piano lessons. Davy signed up for all eight shows at the Met bringing his family an enormous $16 a week for 24 hours of work. He saw show business as a way to keep the family afloat for very little effort. And his negotiating skills were legendary, as evidenced by how he agreed to play Vandgergelder opposite Carol Channing in the original production of *Hello, Dolly!* at the salary he wanted.

Sometimes when we were leaving a restaurant Davy would pull his hat down over his head and become a slobbering drunk. One night as we were walking home from the theater we were passing an arcade on Broadway so I pushed him into a "Four for a Quarter" photo booth, sat down and told him to sit down on my lap and do the drunk. We were coming out of the Alvin Theater one night and a hobo came up to him and ask him for a dime for a cup of coffee. Davy pulled his hat over his ears, started staggering and said to the guy, "A dime? We only did $62,000 last week." (Then he gave him a dollar.)

In 1963, he had just won his second Tony Award for his portrayal of Senex in *Forum*. He was hilarious in the show and at age sixty had reached the top of his profession - the best second banana on Broadway and proud of it.

He told me that Art Carney was the first choice for Vandgergelder followed by Burl Ives. Merrick came to him third. His salary for *Forum* was $1,250 per week and when Merrick offered him Vandgergelder, he offered him the same salary as he got in *Forum*. Davy said he would do the part for $2,000 a week. Merrick countered the offered with fifteen hundred a week and co-star billing above the title with Channing. Davy told Merrick that he didn't give a damn about billing and that his price was two grand. Merrick said no. Davy responded with "Thanks for callin', Dave" and hung up on the great producer.

A few days later Merrick called and offered him a salary of $1,750 if he would sign a one year contract. Davy said, "Dave, I mean this from the bottom of my heart - go fuck yourself," and hung up.

Two days later, Davy got a message from Helen Nickerson, Merrick's secretary, to come to the office on the fourth floor of the St James Theatre on West 44th Street to meet with Merrick face to face. Davy arrived at the appointed time. Helen said he could go right in. Before Davy entered Merrick's office, he took off all his clothes, except for his shoes and socks, then knocked on Merrick's door, walked in with cigar in his cheek and said, "Any casting today?" He got his two grand, and three thousand for every extra year he stayed with the show.

Forum was one of the funniest evenings ever in the theatre. Zero was inspired lunacy and was still having fun early in the run. The first night I saw it, I came out of the Alvin Theatre and went to the stage door to say I wanted to see Mr. Mostel and of course he was expecting me. I lied. The door man told me to go across the stage to the dressing room on the first floor. As I turned to go across the stage, there stood David Burns talking with my father in front of the small elevator.

My father turned and saw me and introduced us. Dad had known him slightly through some Wall Street business. Davy said, "Come on, let's go!" Instead of continuing on to see Zero, I changed course and followed them into the old rickety elevator as they picked up their conversation. The course of my life changed with that left turn.

"I got a lot of Yahoo Chocolate drink," Davy growled.

"I'll look into it," said dad. "But Syntax is promising."

I thought Syntax was some other soft drink as we approached Davy's second floor dressing room but realized that they were talking about stocks. Dad was giving him advice. We walked into his dressing room and the smell took me like an unseen hand and pulled me through the door. It was like a womb. Safe and comfortable. It was a room that had the same comforts as a ten dollar a night hooker hotel room down the street from the theatre. Paint was coming off the walls and there was a solitary sink in the corner.

Without any embarrassment being in front of a complete stranger, Davy took off his costume and continued the conversation stark naked. Dad asked him to join us at Toots Shor's for a late night bite and he accepted. Before we left I asked him to sign my Playbill. He signed my program which said, "Jim, my boy, You are always welcome, Ever lovin' Davy Burns."

I read it and said, "Mr. Burns…."

"DAVE! Call me Dave."

I was a sophomore in high school calling one of my idols "Dave." I said, "Do you mean that?"

He said, "Sure. You're always welcome. Come around any time and I'll talk you out of going into show business."

"But I'm going to be a priest, Dave."

He just looked at me and said, "Well, bless me father I have sinned. Against your will, my child? No against the china cabinet and it would have done your heart good to hear those dishes rattle. Let's eat. I'm in the mood for shad roe."

Over dinner I pelted him with questions about his life. He made his Broadway debut when he was 20, in a play called *Polly Preferred* and went from show to show until his big break in 1939 when he played Banjo, a character based on Harpo Marx in the classic Kaufman and Hart's *The Man who Came To Dinner*. I asked him about Monty Wooley and all he said, as he swallowed his shad roe was, "He was fucking Cole Porter...and he had a very small ass for a fairy."

My father's mouth dropped open -- as did mine. I was a sweet Irish Catholic boy who was going to be a priest and hadn't heard that kind of language except when I was passing by the tough kids on the street corner by the subway. He wasn't anti-gay by any means. It was just his way of talking. He seemed to be far advanced in knowing what made people gay. One night he just simply said, "A chromosome backfired, that's all."

Before we left Toot Shor's that night, I showed him the program where he had signed, "You're always welcome," and I said, "I hope you really mean that." He tousled my hair and said, "I really do." Not a week went by that I didn't see *Forum* and go out with him afterward. Staring at the program when I got home, I knew I would never become a priest. I would live a life in the theatre.

I took Davy at his word and came around to his dressing room whenever I was near the theatre and I made it a habit to be near the theatre every week. Dropping in on Davy had its rewards because you never knew who would be there visiting him - Gene Kelly, Dan Dailey or Howard Keel for instance would be sitting there telling jokes and talking about the old days at MGM.

After a show one night, he told me about playing Ali Hakim in the first road company of "Oklahoma." Later, I heard a famous story about his first day of rehearsal. Reuben Mamoulian, the mercurial director of the show insisted that all actors be on time for rehearsal or they would be fired.

The cast assembled at ten a.m. but Davy was conspicuously absent. A few minutes after ten, he walked onto the stage naked, carrying a large saber, waved the sword around and screamed "What this show needs is some cuts."

Growing up, Davy wanted to be a doctor and he peppered his language with all manner of medical terms. He would tell me that I had a "beautiful medulla oblongata" or "acromegalia of the umbilicus" or "elephantiasis of the lower tarsal" which would send me into hysterics. Once I gave him a towel rack for his birthday that looked like a large dildo. He gave it a prominent place in his dressing room and would pick it up and wave it at visitors.

Davy entertaining school chum George McKay and Press Agent, Al Fields.

Davy was a highly sexual man who had a penchant for Black women -- although any women who would have sex with him would do. When he was doing *Hello, Dolly!* I climbed the steps to his second-floor dressing room before a Saturday matinee, opened the door and found one of the wardrobe women blowing him.

Without missing a beat or showing the slightest bit of embarrassment, he said, "Wait outside, we'll be through in a minute."

He was married to a very beautiful lady named Mildred Todd who had been a dancer in that company of *Oklahoma* where Davy played Ali Hakim. Toddy, as everyone called her, was classy and gracious -- the antithesis of her husband, the devout atheist who believed all religion was a form of mental illness. I remember telling him one night about the Catholic Church's teaching about the Immaculate Conception of the Virgin Mary and he laughed as though I was doing a Henny Youngman routine.

The strange thing about Davy and Toddy's marriage was that she was not only a devout Christian Scientist, she was a practitioner. He, of course, didn't believe in it but always wondered why she was in perfect health and never even caught a cold. The night he won his first Tony Award for playing the blustery Mayor Shinn in *The Music Man* he turned to the audience and said, "Everything I am today I owe to my wife -- who has a lot of money."

In today's politically correct society, Davy would have been brought up on actor's union "charges" at least, or actually jailed for his outrageous, over the top sexual innuendos. I suppose it was in the tradition of the Marx Brothers whose sexual hijacks were also legendary but even the Marx Brothers themselves would be facing prosecution.

The great Broadway character man, George S. Irving told me a story one night about being in a show with Davy who was trying to lure a chorus girl into the sack. He said to her, "Come up and we'll run some lines in my room." The girl arrived to find David in his underwear. She must have known what was going on since it was the middle of winter and no need to sit around in the buff. He started by saying, "Repeat after me. I love your penis." The girl recoiled and repeated the phrase in a horrified manner, adding "David, you're disgusting." He said, "You love my penis and *I'm* disgusting?"

Despite his rather odd behavior off-stage, he was a musical theatre genius who was sought after by every producer in town. He was a good luck charm because, until *Lovely Ladies, Kind Gentlemen* in 1971, he was never in a show that lost money. He could hold his own against any actor that lived -- even the larger-than-life Zero Mostel. Zero and Davy never became friends during the year and a half they spent together in *Forum*. He thought Mostel was a bully who treated Jack Gilford especially badly during the run. Jack would come off the stage covered with bruises having been pummeled all evening by the star. Jack and Zero had been best friends for years and somehow when Jack heard the resulting laugh from being pushed or hit by Zero, he suffered it for the sake of the show.

One night early in the run, Zero put his hands on David thinking that the gesture would get a laugh. It did. As soon as the curtain came down, and in front of the entire cast, David pushed Zero up against the set by his throat and said, "You dirty cocksucker, if you ever do that again I'm going to throw you in the fuckin'
orchestra pit and we'll see if *that* gets a laugh." Zero

never repeated the bit.

Davy said he didn't enjoy working in the theatre. He enjoyed doing commercials and making movies because they only involved "a few days" work and he could go back to the farm. Theatre was a six day work week with the off day exhausted from the previous six.

"Civilians" do not understand what kind of energy it takes to sustain a three hour performance. I've heard, "Well, I work eight hours a day and you only work three." I tell them that if you had to put all that concentrated energy into the eight hours, you'd be dead in a month.

Since his Broadway debut in *Polly Preferred* in 1923, hardly a season went by that David wasn't in a play. He spent three years in England, from 1936 to 1939, and was fast becoming a star of the West End. He co-starred with Gertrude Lawrence in Cole Porter's *Nymph Errant* and then had a major part as George Sanders' sidekick in the RKO picture, *The Saint Over London.*

The 1960s was one of his busiest decades, going from Broadway show to Broadway show without much downtime in between. David and his wife Toddy had a small apartment on East 57th Street but considered their farm in Bucks County to be their true home. Davy loved the East Stroudsburg spread more than anything in the world and treasured the time he could spend there digging and planting. I once asked him what he wanted for his birthday and he said, "Give me a tree."

Just after *Hello, Dolly!* opened in 1964, Davy was honored with a caricature in Sardi's restaurant. Getting a Sardi's caricature is one of the greatest honors an actor can ever receive; to be included on that wall forever with the other great luminaries of the stage. Davy only said, "I always wanted to be hung."

We went to the ceremony where he signed his picture, "For Vincent, All you need is a big stomach and a sense of humor, David Burns." They put his picture up on the wall and there was an empty space right next to it. I had been to Sardi's many times and always felt embraced by the history of that theatrical watering hole. I thought maybe one day my picture would be up there, filling that space right next to Davy. Something to dream about.

But during the sixties, he didn't have a lot of opportunities to spend at the farm except for Sunday, his one night off from the eight-show a week Broadway schedule. The decade began with Davy continuing in his Tony Award winning role as Mayor Shinn in *The Music Man*, leaving that show to play Brains Berman in *Do, Re, Mi*; leaving that show to play Senex in *A Funny Thing Happened on the Way to the Forum* (for which he won his second Tony); leaving that to play Horace Vandergelder in *Hello, Dolly!* opposite Carol Channing, Ginger Rogers and Martha Raye; then leaving that show to play Gregory Solomon in Arthur Miller's *The Price*.

Davy really didn't want to do *The Price*. He had just finished three years in *Dolly* and wanted a break. He also thought the part of Gregory Solomon was too big. Yes, can you imagine an actor who didn't want to take on major starring roles? When Davy was in a show, his ideal part was two scenes – one in the first act and one in the second – where he could come out for ten memorable minutes, steal the scene and then go back to his dressing room and smoke his cigar.

Gregory Solomon was a once-in-a-lifetime role, the part of the 89 year old furniture dealer that has come to buy the remains of a once prosperous family. The two brothers who have inherited the furniture haven't spoken for years. The brother who became a cop (Pat Hingle) had always blamed his successful doctor brother (Arthur Kennedy) for abandoning the family and selfishly following his own dream while forcing him into the dead-end life of a New York City cop. Davy read the play and turned it down flat. He wanted to retire to the country and not work again. Period. He had already turned down Herb Gardner's new play, *The Goodbye People*, because it was the lead and he would have no time off the stage. Milton Berle took the part, the play bombed and closed after seven performances at the Ethel Barrymore Theatre.

But Davy found himself up against two formidable men who found it hard to take "no" for an answer. One was Robert Whitehead, the classiest producer in the history of the American theatre. He had matinee idol good looks, with a silver pompadour, classic Barrymore-esque profile, pencil thin mustache and a dazzling smile that sealed more deals then David Merrick's glares. He was a down to earth, approachable man who was married to the great actress, Zoe Caldwell. The second man who wanted Davy in the part was the author of the piece, Arthur Miller. Miller always got what he wanted.

Individually, they approached Davy who said the part was much too big and he was too tired. He hadn't had a breather since 1956. They offered to push back the start of rehearsals to give him a little respite after his long stretch with *Dolly*. It was when they offered him $5,000 a week that the poor boy from the lower East side saw it as an offer he couldn't refuse and he agreed.

The cast would be Jack Warden as the policeman, Victor Franz; Kate Reid as his wife, Esther; Arthur Kennedy (whom everyone called Jack) as Walter Franz and Davy as Gregory Solomon. The understudies were not stars but all were first rate actors; Eugene Roche (the grease-cutting cook from the Ajax commercials) would cover Warden, Arthur Miller's sister Joan Copeland would stand by for Reid; Paul Sparer would understudy Kennedy and an old friend of Davy's named Harold Gary would cover him. Ulu Grosbard would direct.

Rehearsals began in November of 1967 at the New Amsterdam Theatre roof. Davy and I would have dinner at the day's end and I would meet him at the theatre at 7 pm and we would go to Schrafft's or Sardi's or sometimes just Nathan's at the corner of 43rd and Broadway for a hot dog. I would start getting to the Roof earlier and earlier and by the end of the first week, I was arriving at four – after my college classes – and sit quietly in the back watching the great icons of the American Theatre putting together a new play. And things weren't going well.

The rehearsal space was the empty shell of the legendary roof theatre of the New Amsterdam, now gloriously refurbished, but then a musky, dusty shell of its former glory. As I sat in the back, I could just imagine the spectacle of the gowned women and tuxedoed men who once would flock to the roof after the theatre for

Ziegfeld's late night revues. There were a few chairs, where once, rows of candle lit tables hosted New York's glitterati and on the stage, the floor of the set was represented with pieces of tape and scattered prop pieces where the real ones would be.

It was a cold place – not only in temperature but in terms of the relationship between the cast, the playwright and the director. Ulu Grosbard was a Belgian who spoke in a slightly Germanic accent but carried the full weight of a Prussian autocrat. He had come to prominence a few years earlier as the director of Frank Gilroy's memory play, *The Subject Was Roses*.

Jack Warden, as the cop, was never off the stage from the curtain's rise to its fall. He and Grosbard had very different styles of working, Warden from the inside out and Grosbard from the outside in. Miller was not too fond of Grosbard's style either and soon the two men were fighting, with Warden caught in the middle. Arthur Miller was a very down-to-earth man who was extremely frustrated with Grosbard's direction. Grosbard would give the actor a motivation and Miller would say, "Wait! Ulu, could I see you for a minute." Grosbard and Miller would then go off to the side, leaving the cast to mumble among themselves. Grosbard would then come back with a totally different take from what he had just said. Many times, Jack Warden would throw his script down and bark, "Will you two make up your minds."

Ten days before the troupe was to leave for their Philadelphia engagement, Warden had had it and asked to be released. I guess the powers that be knew that Warden was going to leave because the next day Pat Hingle was on board and almost off book. Hingle's arrival eased some of the tension but not between Miller and Grosbard. Miller would sit a few feet away from me with Del Hughes, a former actor turned stage manager and keep a close eye on the script. Grosbard would give the cast a direction and almost immediately Miller would countermand it. By the last week of rehearsals, Grosbard was sitting with the stage manager and Miller was directing his own play.

The understudies would also watch rehearsal and take notes. Davy sat down with Harold Gary who said, "I don't know why they brought me on to cover you. They're wasting their money -- you never get sick. I'm as useless as the pope's prick."

"Well," Davy said, "You never need a fireman until there's a fire." His words would prove prophetic, for the blaze would break out ten days later. After rehearsal, Davy and I walked to Schrafft's at 43rd Street and Broadway with Hal Gary. He joined us for a soda. Davy always ordered the Schrafft's "Broadway Soda" which was made of chocolate soda and coffee ice cream. Hal ordered a pineapple soda. I never spoke to Mr. Gary before this as he always looked rather grumpy and unapproachable. He was bemoaning the fact that here he was in his mid-sixties and still an understudy. He and his brother Sid Gary had done a vaudeville act just as the medium was dying and Hal went on to a career of bit parts, standing by for other actors or replacing them when they got tired of the part. And here he was doing it again. Davy never missed a show. Ever.

Later that week the company went to Philadelphia to start their out of town tryout at the Walnut Street Theatre. I followed a few days later; Davy had gotten me a ticket for the Saturday matinee. He was happy that he didn't have to shave because the character didn't have to shave. I hung out in the dressing room with him until half-hour. During that time, Ulu Grosbard came in with notes – the major one being that he thought Davy could pick up the pace. A few minutes later Arthur Miller poked his head in and assured Davy he didn't have to rush anything and he could take his time. Davy just shook his head.

I thought the show was breathtaking. Pat Hingle, although unsteady in some scenes and needing a line or two thrown to him, was clearly going to be brilliant in the part. Jack Kennedy, Kate Reid and Davy were magnificent. The play was a little long and Miller and Grosbard were having differences as to whether or not the show should be played with an intermission. There was no logical break in the action, was Miller's point. Both Grosbard and Bob Whitehead thought that the audience needed a break. Miller relented and allowed the intermission to occur as soon as the long lost brother (Kennedy) appears at the door. Hingle would just look at the door; see his brother and say, "Walter!"

Curtain. The meat of the play came in act two with the theme being hammered home that one pays a price for every decision one makes in life. The "Price" was not just the price old Solomon would pay for the furniture; it was about the price one paid for the choices one makes. The play was very compelling and the audiences loved it. So did I.

I was heading backstage after to see Davy when I found myself going through the door with Arthur Miller. He said, "So what do you think?" I said, "I think it's great, Mr. Miller." He smiled and said, "It'll get better." I learned a great lesson about theatre that day – a legendary playwright will ask anyone for their opinion.

Back in New York, I saw the second preview of the show and Davy gave a superb performance. Both Whitehead and Miller came back to his dressing room and congratulated him for nailing it. They were ready to face the New York critics. After the show, we walked to Schrafft's. Davy's mood was decidedly downbeat. Max Eisen, the publicist, was with us and did most of the talking. Instead of his "Broadway" ice cream soda, Davy ordered tea and toast, saying that his stomach was upset and that the toast would help settle it.

Instead of walking, Davy uncharacteristically took a cab back to his apartment at 57th Street and 2nd Avenue while I took the RR subway back to Bay Ridge. The next night my father came home around midnight with the next morning's edition of the *Daily News*. I opened to the theater page and there saw the boxed article with the headline: "David Burns out of *The Price* after surgery." Even though it was after midnight, I instinctively picked up the phone and called David's house. Toddy answered. She was awake and could hear the panic in my voice. "What happened?"

"Yesterday morning," she started, "David woke up in a great deal of pain. I took him to the doctor who ordered him to the hospital immediately. When they took x-rays, they discovered his colon had burst and peritonitis was setting in fast. He almost died, Jim, but they saved him."

"When can I see him?" I begged.
"It will be a few weeks, Jim. He's very sick."
"But he's going to be all right?"
"Yes, he'll be fine."
I don't know why this next question was important but I blurted out, "Will he go back to the show?"

Toddy said she doubted it. A few nights later, *The Price* opened at the Morosco Theatre with Harold Gary in the part. When Gary made his first entrance, I gasped because he looked and sounded so much like David. He went on to get enthusiastic reviews for a finely nuanced performance but in essence he was only doing an imitation of David and the character he had so vividly brought to life.

Two days later, I sneaked into Cedars Sinai Hospital and up to his room on the second floor. He was alone and in far worse shape than I imagined. He was half in and half out of consciousness, obviously still in a tremendous amount of pain. I took his hand and he mumbled, "Bless me father…"

"How are you?"

"Bad. My gluteus maximus is attached to my tonsils now." Then he fell asleep. I sat with him as he slept for an hour and then I left. A few nights later, I came back and found he was sitting up in bed, eating Jell-O.

"I hate fucking Jell-O!"

"Then fuck one of the nurses instead," I told him.

He grabbed his side, "Jesus! Don't make me laugh. I can't laugh."

David was not a natural laugher to begin with. Like so many of the vaudeville comics who were his contemporaries, he could hear the most hilarious joke ever told and just say, "That's funny."

One of the nurses came in and said, "Don't you want to watch the president?" We had both forgotten that Lyndon Johnson was making an important announcement and he was about to come on television.

"Sure," Davy growled, "Let's see what the cocksucker has to say."

Just as the nurse pushed the remote control button, Davy let burst a thunderous fart -- except that it came from his belly. Although he had his pajamas and bed covering over it, the sound was deafening. It lasted what seemed like hours. He was clearly embarrassed -- an emotion I thought he was incapable of -- because it confirmed that he had undergone a colostomy.

"Thar' she blows," he covered.

Johnson came on the television and announced that "he would not seek nor would he accept the nomination of his party for another term as president."

"Fuckin' war did him in," Davy observed. The "fuckin' war" was the Vietnam conflict which was taking its toll both physically and morally on the country. Kennedy had gotten us into it and Johnson couldn't get us out -- without "losing face."

The war scared the hell out of me because I was the right age. I had a student deferment which would be running out in a year. I got my "greetings" letter the year before and had to go to a dismal army center near the Battery to have my physical. When it came time to "check the box" about being homosexual, I bravely checked it and then erased it, then check and erased it again, so that there a small hole where the check should be.

There didn't seem to be much of a chance I was going to be drafted as I weighed 325 pounds and the army didn't have a uniform to fit me. Even after my draft lottery number was called, a low 44, the army never sought me out. I lost friends in Viet Nam who went believing that they were fighting for their country's freedom. Now, as I write, I just received an email from a friend on a cruise in Viet Nam who tells me the shopping is excellent.

Davy was in the hospital for almost a month and every week Robert Whitehead visited him and told him that he wanted him to come back to the show. Davy said he didn't want to, but I could tell he really did.

Pat Hingle, who replaced Jack Warden in the part of Victor Franz remembers putting *The Price* together as an exercise in near chaos. Hingle told me, "Jack Warden got sick. Arthur Miller took over the direction. They postponed the opening to give me more time to get up in the part and then Davy got sick. It was not like *Dark At The Top of the Stairs* which didn't have a line change from the very beginning. From the time the curtain went up in New Haven to New York, it was a hit. Gangbusters! But in *The Price* you hardly passed one crisis without having "another."

Hingle also went to visit David at Mount Sinai and was surprised to see a very vulnerable side. "I went up to say "Hi," Hingle said, "and I knew a lot about hospitals. I had talked to the doctor before I saw him, who told me that the operation, although extensive, was not terribly serious and David would have a full recovery. Davy had never been in a hospital before and he had cast himself as a man who wasn't going to live to leave it. He had made up his mind that he was sick and dying and why was he in the hospital if he wasn't dying. But I said to him, 'You son of a bitch, you're going to die in a cotton field at the age of 102 because you're a peasant.'

He stopped playing the role of invalid and started to get better, but some of the nurses told me it was easier to deal with the invalid.

A date of June 15th, four months after his surgery, was selected for him to replace his own replacement and return to *The Price* as Gregory Solomon.

Toddy was away at the beginning of June and Davy asked if I would come to the country, stay overnight and run lines with him to help get him back into the part. We ran lines well into the night. I was playing the cop and soon, we were performing the piece rather than just running lines. Before we went to bed he said, "You know, you're a good actor."

We watched TV for a while, saw Bobby Kennedy's acceptance speech for winning the California primary and went to bed. I slept in Toddy's bed in their bedroom and when I woke up the next morning, Davy's bed was empty. I went down to the kitchen and found him in his pajamas and robe, standing at the counter in front of a small television that was tuned to *The Today Show*. He was sobbing uncontrollably. I had never seen him cry, much less sob. He sensed I was behind him and through his sobbing said, "The poor son of a bitch is dead. Goddammit!"

I focused on the television and saw the picture of Robert F. Kennedy. He had been shot in the basement kitchen of the Ambassador Hotel in Los Angeles immediately after his winning the California Presidential primary. Just ten weeks before, I had a face to face encounter with the Senator on St. Patrick's Day.

I enjoyed marching in the St. Patrick's Day parade first with my high school and then with St. Francis College. In the 1968 parade, I was chosen to hold our banner in the front of the group. When our unit got to the corner of 44th Street and Fifth Avenue, we were stopped

as we heard a commotion to our left. Bobby Kennedy was

going to march in front of us. He was our Senator and he was running for president and in my opinion he was going to win. For the entire parade route, he marched ten feet in front of us.

David Burns, Garson Kanin, Maureen Stapleton and me.

It was thrilling the way the crowd reacted to him, screaming and cheering, reaching out to him like a savior. He waved back at them, melting the frosty March air with his dazzling smile. When we got to the corner of 82nd Street and 5th Avenue, he stopped waving and started blowing kisses toward an apartment house on the East side of the Street. I followed his hand and saw in a second or third floor window Jacqueline Kennedy Onassis beaming back at him and returning the kisses with a wave.

When we got to the corner of 86th Street, RFK was at once surrounded by his aides and Secret Service as they started to lead him to a waiting car. Before he went, he turned back to our group and starting with me, shook all of our hands. "Er, thanks for letting me march with you. St. Francis is a fine school. Great basketball team." He had my vote. It was as big a thrill to meet him as it had been to meet his brother so many years before. Sadly, he would experience the same fate as his brother a mere three months later.

Harold Gary was angry that Davy was coming back. He had gotten good reviews for his performance though the Broadway community denied him a Tony Award nomination because, although he opened in the show, most felt he was a replacement. On June 15, 1968, David returned to *The Price* and got the praise he so richly deserved for his outstanding performance.

Producer David Susskind asked David to recreate Gregory Solomon for the television version of *The Price*, the only member of the original cast. It was being presented by the Hallmark Hall of Fame and starring George C. Scott, Colleen Dewhurst and Barry Sullivan. David flew to London where the show was filmed as a play, just as it had been done on Broadway.

Davy and George Scott loved each other right off the bat and Davy would spend off-stage hours teaching Scott old vaudeville routines. Scott's ex-wife, Dewhurst, would sip a martini and roar watching them do routine after routine between takes.

Susskind knew that he wanted Davy for the part from the beginning and also knew that Davy drove a hard bargain. According to Susskind, "He was meticulous about money and what he thought he was worth. In the negotiations, he didn't suffer agents. You talked to him directly because he didn't like people taking ten percent of his money.

He told me that if he didn't get his price for *The

Price he wasn't interested. I told him that he had to play the part. It would be his monument. He didn't want to spend three months in London to shoot it and he wanted ten thousand dollars. Finally, Susskind compromised. We would rehearse the film in New York and shoot in London and he would get $7,500 with $2,500 in expenses. He knew expenses weren't taxed."

Susskind said that shooting *The Price* in England was, unlike mounting the Broadway production, a total joy. "Between takes," he added, "Davy and George C. Scott would do these burlesque sketches and mincing. They danced and sang and it was a lark. George adored Davy." Susskind was right; the television version of *The Price* was a monument to David's genius as an actor.

When the Emmys were handed out the next year, David won for Best Supporting Actor in a drama. The award was presented by Lucille Ball and Jack Benny. Toddy accepted for Davy who had died only a month before. When Davy returned to the States he came to see me in a musical I was doing at Lincoln Center called *Skye*.

It was a delightful fantasy written by Avery Corman who went on to write *Kramer Versus Kramer*. A charming show, I played a singing dancing dragon named MacDuff. My costume had a huge tail that swung with my hips and it was one of the funniest parts I ever played. Davy came backstage afterwards and said, "Well, you're very good but there's not a lot of dragon parts around these days."

Though he swore he was going to retire, he was asked to do a new musical by Kander and Ebb based on Peter Coke's play *A Breath of Spring* which had been adapted for the screen as part of the British "Carry-On Gang's" film of *Make Mine Mink*. The premise of *70,*

Girls, 70 was that a group of retired vaudevillians, faced with eviction from their home, take to stealing mink coats in order to survive. David, even though he always said he didn't want to do any more Broadway shows, took the part when Eddie Foy Jr. was fired during rehearsals.

Davy rehearsed in New York before joining the show in its Forrest Theatre, Philadelphia tryout. The Forrest Theatre is one of the most beautiful in the country, built in the 1920's with one enormous flaw. When the theatre was finished, someone noticed that they had forgotten to include dressing rooms in the blueprints. The owners had to buy the house in back of the theatre and then build an underground tunnel to connect the theatre to the house, which then had to be converted to dressing rooms.

I drove Davy to Philadelphia for his first show. We sat in the empty auditorium and watched a rehearsal of the second act opening called "You Old Bastard." The youngest person in the cast was 64 with most of them in their 70s and a few in their 80s. John Kander was on the stage near the piano while Fred Ebb paced nervously up and down the aisle. Every once in a while he would confer with Paul Aaron, the director. Things were not going well. The four "altacockers" in the number were having trouble being a "rock band" singing over and over again, "You Old Bastard." Davy looked at me and said, "Kind of makes you believe in death, doesn't it?" Then it was Davy's turn to rehearse his number - a charming duet with the only youngster in the cast, Tommy Breslin, playing the bellboy of the hotel. *Go Visit Your Grandmother* was going to be the highlight/showstopper of act two and everyone knew it.

The show was struggling to find a tone and this song embodied everything the show should be.

Paul Aaron, the director, was in over his head and using hubris instead of brains to steer his actors. When Davy and Tommy finished the number, Aaron, standing in the third row of the orchestra said, "That was good, but David -- let me show you how to get a laugh here." You could hear the rest of the cast gasp out loud. Paul knew he had crossed a line though he didn't know what he had done. Every veteran in the cast stopped and watched Paul come to the stage and make a suggestion, to which Davy with a wry smile said, "Okay, Paul, show me how to get a laugh." But what the cast, including costars Mildred Natwick and Lillian Roth, were trying to tell their neophyte director was that telling David Burns how to get a laugh was like telling the pope how to say mass.

The show was received tepidly in its out of town tryout and changes were being made every day. It was rough on the older cast to be playing the show at night and rehearsing new material for five hours every afternoon. Paul Aaron was replaced by the more experienced Stanley Prager who still couldn't get a handle on the material but at least gave it some cohesion and energy.

I was going to drive to Philadelphia with my friend Mary Jo Catlett for the evening show on March 12, 1971. We would stay over, see both shows on Saturday and drive back with Davy. Just before I was about to leave, Mary Jo called and said she didn't want to spend the night in Philly and could we go early in the morning instead? I was going to share Davy's room at the Sylvania Hotel but Mary Jo was going to have to find a place to crash so I understood. "Sure," I said, "we'll go in the morning."

I called David around four p.m. at his hotel room. He didn't sound sick, but he did sound very tired. I told him we wouldn't be there that night and we would see him late the next morning. He told me he had ordered a sandwich from room service and was going to go back to the theatre early to get a nap before the show. He never slept well at night but could always fall asleep better on a cot at the theatre than in a bed at the hotel.

About eleven o'clock that night, the phone rang. It was Mary Jo. She was crying. Tommy Breslin had just called her. Davy was dead. He died of a heart attack after their big number. In the middle of a scene where the old folks were pretending to be ill, Davy collapsed of a massive cardiac arrest. He fell behind a couch and the audience thought it was part of the show and howled as he was dragged into the wings. The last two sounds he ever heard were laughter and applause.

I drove to Philadelphia the next day as I had planned, crying all the way down the New Jersey Turnpike. I got to the theatre about eleven a.m. and went through the stage door. The doorman knew me well enough by that time not only to let me through but to offer his condolences. Davy's understudy, Coley Worth, was on stage getting ready to go on for the matinee. I watched from the wings as he did the scenes with Mildred Natwick and then ran the number with Tommy. I could see John Kander and Fred Ebb sitting in the orchestra like zombies, as if they still couldn't believe what had happened the night before.

Rehearsal was over and the actors headed for the elevator which would take them downstairs to the basement where they could traverse the underground passage to their dressing rooms. Mildred Natwick saw me standing there as she passed, took my hand and said, "Come on. You look like you need to talk."

We went downstairs and crossed over and then up to her dressing room. Her dresser was there. She dismissed her and closed the door. All I could say was "What happened?"

Miss Natwick was upset but she also needed to talk about it. It all poured out of her. "I knew he was dead," she started. "I knew it right away. And then I had to go out and sing *The Elephant Song*. (Ironically, a song about death.) And I knew. He just fell over. He did the joke about needing an operation and he pulled his shirt up and just fell over. The audience screamed. Coley (Worth) and Joey (Faye) dragged him off stage and the audience just kept laughing and then they applauded. They didn't know it wasn't part of the show. And when they got him into the wings, Coley started to pound him on the chest and then a doctor came and saw Coley pounding on his chest but Coley was wearing his policeman's uniform -- it was a costume -- but the doctor thought he was really a policeman and didn't act right away.

They thought he was a cop doing CPR but he wasn't. He was just pounding on his chest. But David was dead. I knew he was dead. Then Arthur Whitelaw (the producer) came back and everyone came back to help and then the ambulance came and took him to Jefferson Hospital. It's right across the street but it didn't matter. It was too late. He was dead. And then I had to go out and sing that damn song. The show was still going on. Nothing stopped. Lillian spoke David's lines and nobody in the audience really knew until the end of the show when David didn't come out for his curtain call. But no one made an announcement.

Nobody said anything. When I came out of the stage door last night, there was a small crowd looking for autographs and no one said anything except there were two ladies there and they didn't want an autograph. They just said, "He's dead, isn't he?"

She finally took a breath and added, "I'm so sorry."

I hugged her and started to leave. Then she said, "Have you spoken to Mrs. Burns yet?" I told her I hadn't. It seems that Arthur Whitelaw sent two state troopers to be at their East Stroudsburg farm when he called to tell her what had happened. I heard she was very calm about the news, but then, as a Christian Scientist she believed he was in a better place.

During the matinee, I sat with Nancy Andrews who was the cover for both Mildred Natwick and Lillian Roth. The news had hit the street that morning and the matinee was sold out -- some just coming to see what would happen without Davy on the stage. As the house lights went down, the stage manager's voice came over the public address system: "At this performance, the role of Harry, usually played by David Burns, will be played by Coley Worth. The audience applauded wildly, encouraging Coley and giving David one final round. At the end of the show, Coley took the penultimate bow and then stepped back into his chorus position leaving an empty space where Davy would have stood. Coley was being respectful to his old friend, at the same time symbolically saying that no one could take David Burns place.

70 Girls 70 opened on Broadway in April 1971 with Hans Conried in David's part, a week after Stephen Sondheim's *Follies* debuted. It was roundly panned. Strange, since the audiences truly loved it and gave it a standing ovation almost every night.

In the meantime, David won the Emmy Award for his role in the television version of *The Price*, the first actor to do so posthumously. Toddy accepted and thanked David Susskind, the producer who had faith in him, Arthur Miller who wrote the part and the castmates that he adored. It was his only Broadway performance that was ever recorded.

A month after Davy's death, a memorial service was held at the 46th Street Theatre. The theatre, now the Richard Rodgers, was filled to overcapacity -- standing room only. Jackie Gleason sat in the last row, along with George Abbott and David Merrick. On stage was Arthur Miller, Jack Gilford, Fred Ebb and a host of others who had worked with Davy and loved him. George C. Scott was the last to speak and brought down the house with the line, "Well, wherever Davy is now he's laughing his ass off 'cause he died in Philadelphia."

I could hear someone weeping behind me. It was Jackie Gleason

Davy is sitting on my lap in a Times Square Photo Booth doing his drunk act.

CHAPTER FOUR
Pyramids, Players and Pipe Nights

Dad and I taking a camel ride at the Pyramids in Giza, Egypt 1962. The camel driver's name was Moses Schwartz. It was free to ride but cost $20.00 to get off. Notice how dad wears his fez at a jaunty angle.

I was twenty-five years old and still living with my father in the two bedroom Bay Ridge apartment in which I grew up. I felt guilty living with him at that age. All my other twenty-five year old friends were out on their own but I still lived with my parent. Since my mother died when I was two, dad and I had become more like older and younger brothers.

It had been only the two of us for years and so it seemed like a good and very livable arrangement. Most of my friends were on their own because they hated their parents and couldn't stand living with them for another minute. I actually enjoyed living with my dad - most of the time.

He also loved to travel and so by the age of fifteen, I had already been halfway around the world. Dad and I began traveling when I was six; a trip to Miami Beach, Florida during Easter vacation which became an annual event. Just dad and me. In 1954, air travel was a thrilling and luxurious experience. People would dress in their nicest clothes; some women would have their hair done for the flight and men would be shaved and scented. It was on the flight to Miami that I met my first celebrity, though I had no idea who she was.

When we arrived for the check in – the whole family came to see us off – the lady behind the counter told us that Irene Dunne would be on our flight. A few minutes later, Miss Dunne appeared and everyone in the waiting area applauded. As she walked by, she looked at me and said, "You look sharp, mister." My father had dressed me in a sport coat and even made me wear a porkpie hat which I thought looked stupid. I guess Irene Dunne disagreed.

It was our third trip to Miami Beach that was life changing – I was a nine year old boy discovering his passion and passions – my first time singing in front of a large audience and my first time fooling around with another nine year old boy. Yes, nine. Like Federico Fellini.

    We stayed at the same hotel every year, the President Madison on 39th and Collins Avenue in the heart of Miami Beach. It was a two story, U-shaped building with stucco white walls that enveloped a large pool, Tiki bar and was steps form the ocean. There was a voluptuous social director named Ruth Roney who conducted most of the daytime activities in a tiger-striped bikini and emceed the shows at night in a low-cut frock. . I wondered why she spent a lot of time with my father or why he had to tuck her into bed after he had done the same for me.

Ruth, dad and I were on an outing to the dog races, driving in her convertible. I was in the backseat singing up a storm. Ruth told me I had a good voice and wanted me to sing in the "Hotel Guest Amateur Show." That night I was onstage in front of a few hundred people. My choice of song? "La Vie En Rose." What? "La Vie En Rose?" Here I was nine years old singing a passionate "La Vie En Rose" like Edith Piaf. But the audience roared in approval when I finished and I had my first dose of the most powerful drug of all – applause.

Speaking of firsts, there was a kid who became a good pal during our stay, a nice Jewish boy from Brooklyn named Gary Cohen. I use his real name because there has to be a thousand Gary Cohens in the country and I'll never forget him. He was about a month younger but old and wise in the ways of sex. One afternoon after swimming, we were in my room changing and he saw my dick "Wow," he said, "I've never seen one like that before!" Of course, Jewish boys were circumcised and I was not.

He asked if he could see it up close? Before I could say no (I wouldn't have anyway) he took it in his hand and began playing with it. I reciprocated. The next thing you know we were two naked kids going around on the bed and that was the beginning of it all. I liked it. He found the solarium on the roof of the hotel where men sunbathed nude. Our after lunch routine was swimming, watching naked men (and counting the cut from the uncut) then stupid nun tried to teach us that such things were wrong and I'd be going to hell. Didn't believe it then, don't believe it now. Neither of us could orgasm but there was a joyful innocence about it all.

Then Dad thought it would be a good idea for my social future if I took dancing lessons. So after Gary and I would explore each other, I would take a half hour dance class. I loved it. My teacher looked like Delores Del Rio and the class ended with a show in the main room featuring all the students. My big number was "Cherry Pink and Apple Blossom White."

In 1960 we took our first cruise to South America. The next year, we were on the M.S. Bergensfjord for a cruise to the Baltic and Russia. Russia was a very closed society and I always felt like we were being watched. In Moscow, we stayed at the Hotel Leningradskaya where there was a massive, severe looking woman stationed on every floor by the elevator.

She would take you to your room, open the door and then lock you in until you called to be released.

We were taken to Lenin's tomb which, at that time, he shared with Joseph Stalin. We entered the tomb, carved out of the Kremlin Wall bordering Red Square, and walked down miles of marble steps, the temperature dropping with each step. We reached bottom and turned into a small, dark room where Lenin and Stalin were lying side by side, looking like two wax figures.

Our traveling companion for the three days in Moscow was Ethel Strouse, the mother of Broadway composer Charles Strouse. She was a lovely, outgoing lady with a deep, rumbling laugh that filled a room. The food in Moscow was just awful. We were told to stay away from any milk products as they were not pasteurized. At dinner on the last night, Mrs.

Dad in Red Square standing in front of Lenin's tomb at the Kremlin. (1961)

Strouse was so hungry and fed up at the same time that she dove into a bowl of ice cream. She came across some unidentifiable chips through and asked out loud, "Does anyone know what these are?" My father said, "Yes, they are big frozen tubercular germs." Ethel laughed her uproarious roar and kept on eating. "Well," she said, "they're the only edible thing I've had since we landed in this damn country."

We flew back to Leningrad (now St. Petersburg again) and as the ship sailed the band on the shore played *God Bless America* and both the Americans on board and the Russians on the shore cried.

Then we cruised the Mediterranean countries in 1962 on the American Export ship, S.S. *Atlantic*. I got to ride a camel at the Pyramids and even passed out in Jerusalem at the tomb of King David on Mount Zion. The temperature was one hundred and twenty degrees and I hadn't eaten. I could feel the fainting spell come on and I laid down on the hot stones before I fell on them. I announced to the people I was with very calmly, "I'm fainting now" and slipped into unconsciousness. The next thing I knew, someone had filled a large hat with water and threw it on my face. Living with dad had its advantages. I was one lucky human being and I knew it.

Dad looked like a cross between the Duke of Windsor and Jimmy Stewart - a dashing Wall Street bond trader who hated his job. He carefully chose his wardrobe each morning, meticulously matching tie and pocket handkerchief. He had a nervous habit of going to the bathroom at least four times in six minutes before he left. He really didn't want to go to work but still got into the waiting limo and drove off through the Brooklyn Battery Tunnel - a dream he had helped to realize by selling the bonds that funded the project.

All the neighbors thought we were tediously rich because he rode in a limo, but the truth of the matter was that dad's friend Buddy Wallace owned the limo and drove to Wall Street each morning anyway. He just took dad along for the company and the price of the tolls. Friday night was known as dad's "night to howl." All the pent-up hatred of the business that imprisoned him welled up on Friday night and sent him uptown for his three regular stops of progressive drunkenness on the New York night scene that I started to call the "Hot Triangle." Every Friday night at 8:15 sharp he would leave his Wall Street hangout, The Coachman, and drive with Buddy Wallace uptown to Sardi's on West 44th Street, then to Toots Shor's on East 52nd and then close out the night at Jilly's nightclub on West 52nd. Buddy would wait for him and drive him back to Brooklyn. Buddy, an ex-prizefighter, was as punchy as they come. Dad would usually get home about three in the morning totally plotzed. Lots of Fridays I would meet him downtown then drive with him to Sardi's, see a show and catch up with him at Jilly's.

Jilly's was right next to the Alvin Theatre where I first met Zero while he was doing Forum. Zero Mostel considered himself a painter who acted rather than an actor who painted. In July of 1977, Mostel left his art studio on 28th street and began rehearsals to star as Shylock in Arnold Wesker's drama, The Merchant. He would only play one performance in Philadelphia before his untimely death on September 8th at the age of sixty-two. When I heard the news I thought back to the day when I first met the larger-than-life star. It was 1962. I was a sophomore in high school, enamored with the theatre and lucky enough to have a mentor like David Burns. I had no idea who Zero Mostel was when I first saw Forum but was knocked out by the comedic force of nature that ruled over the stage of the Alvin Theatre.

I made my way backstage to see Davy and literally ran into Mostel who looked like he had just taken a shower in his costume – steamy and covered with sweat. I was attending military school and dressed in my West Point style uniform which caught his attention. "You must be General Nuisance. What do you want?" he snorted. "I'm here to see Davy Burns," I said.

"You never come to see me!" he grunted.

"I will," I said as he brushed past me and disappeared down the dark hallway

The next week, I saw the show again, visited Davy and then went to Zero's dressing room. He was reading the riot act to one of the actors who he thought had upstaged him. The funny man I loved onstage had become a screaming maniac and all I could do was stand back and cringe. The actor apologized and left. Zero looked at me with exploding eyes and said, "What do you want?"

"To say hello," I managed to articulate.

His rage turned to total charm in a nanosecond.

"Well, hello! Come in." I sat in his dressing room as he asked me all sorts of questions - like why was I a fat kid in a military uniform? From that night until he left the show, whenever I came to visit Davy, I always spent time with Zero too. Once, I asked Zero for an autographed photo which I never received. Years later, after I got my first Off-Broadway show, *Unfair to Goliath*, I ran into Zero in front of the Winter Garden Theatre at Broadway and 50th Street. I told him I was now a professional actor to which he replied, "I'll be the judge of that." I jokingly reminded him that I had asked him for an autographed picture eight years before and still hadn't gotten it. Zero looked at me in his crazy, insane way, screamed, "You're not worthy!" and walked away. The next day my disappointment turned to joy when I arrived at the Cherry Lane Theatre and found a manila envelope waiting for me. Inside was a picture of Zero inscribed, "To Jimmy with my Admiration, Zero Mostel."

I used to refer to David Burns as my "Uncle" because he was like a second father to me. My own father was an alcoholic - although like James Dunn in *A Tree Grows in Brooklyn*, a charming one. I always joked that I never knew my father drank until I saw him sober. I didn't know how Davy would feel about my calling him an "Uncle" but found out one day when he took me to The Players Club on Gramercy Park. We ran into a fellow I met there once who looked at Davy and said, "Oh yes, I've met your nephew." My stomach froze for a moment because I didn't know how he would react to my lie. After a beat Davy looked at him and said, "Good, so I don't have to introduce you."

The Players Club is a time-honored club for us theatrical types founded in 1886. My first time there was in December of 1969. I was just starting out in show business and auditioning for everything whether I was right or wrong for the part. And all I wanted was to get an Equity card to work with the pros. There was a casting call in "Backstage Magazine" for a production of *The Taming of the Shrew* that was actually being done on a Broadway Production contract and playing over the forthcoming Christmas holiday at Town Hall on West 43rd Street.

The open cattle call was being held at the Jerry LeRoy studios on 8th Avenue and 46th Street. There were hundreds of people squeezed into a small, moldy hallway being herded by a frazzled, wild-eyed woman trying to keep it all together. She couldn't. I found out later that she was Jeanne Slon, wife of the producer-director Sidney Slon, who had been pressed into service to help out. Sidney Slon made his reputation as one of the writers of the radio classic *The Shadow* and had always wanted to direct Shakespeare on Broadway.

Actors were given numbers after they presented their Equity cards, but I sat back and watched since I wasn't a member of the union and was going to wait until the end of the call to try to be seen. Suddenly, Jeanne Slon came out of the audition room shouting, "Next ten! Next ten! Quickly, quickly please!" She didn't seem to be checking cards or any kind of order so I went in with nine other guys to be given the once-over by Mr. Slon.

He kept looking at me, perhaps because I was six feet four inches and weighed over three hundred pounds - a standout in any crowd. He scanned the line, dismissed the other nine men and asked me to read the opening speech. He smiled, said "Very good" and then asked me how old I was (a practice that one would be fined for doing at an audition today.) I told him I had just turned twenty-three and he said I was far too young for the role, "Thanks for coming." Before I left, I slipped my picture and resume into his briefcase and made my way into the outside room which looked like a refugee camp.

Two weeks later, at seven in the morning, the phone rang. It was Sidney Slon. He told me that they had started rehearsals for *Shrew* and the actor he had picked for the part was not working out. He was very proud that he had seen "something" in me at the audition and had deliberately "saved" my picture and resume. Could I meet him at the Players Club for lunch at noon. I was excited but overcome with fear that I had sneaked into an Equity audition and was about to be found out.

I was fifteen minutes early for my appointment and I waited outside of 16 Gramercy Park South on a freezing November day so that I could walk into the club at the stroke of noon. I looked up at the great impressive sandstone building, marveling that this was the home of one of the greatest actors in American history, Edwin Booth, the brother of Lincoln's assassin, John Wilkes.

As the first bell struck noon, I opened the great oak door bearing the seal of The Players and walked up the five marble steps to the first landing. A huge fireplace dominated the room over which a portrait of the great Edwin Booth himself loomed above, greeting everyone who entered. Sid Slon was sitting on one of the red overstuffed couches facing the door and leapt up when he saw me. He couldn't have been nicer, greeting me like a veteran actor rather than the tyro I was.

"Come, let's have lunch!" he half-ordered, half-invited, "I'll give you the tour later." We walked into the dining room and took a table for two against the dark, wood paneled wall. Sidney was a tall sturdy fellow, very stately, somewhat British looking, a man with the face of a butler and the bearing of a prime minister. He began by saying that the show had started rehearsals a few days before and the actor to whom he had given the part returned the favor by giving him nothing but attitude, problems and grief. Of course I assured him right away that I was extremely easy to work with.

He handed me the script and asked me to read a few lines out loud. I only got a few words out when he said, "Very good. Nice interpretation. You'll do well. We can age you up a bit." He told me the salary was $156 per week, a Broadway contract. Then he added almost as an afterthought, "You are a member of Equity, aren't you?"

I didn't know whether to shit or go blind at that moment but something told me to tell the truth and let the Equity cards fall where they may. I said, "No, Mr. Slon, I'm not." Without batting an eye he responded, "Well, you'll have to join. Would you like some dessert?

I signed my Equity contract and reported to Town Hall for rehearsal at four p.m. I was the first there, and like the times I walked through the stage door I sold orange drink at Broadway theatres during high school, I was filled with that wonderful, heady aroma of backstage. The doorman welcomed me and said I was the first - as usual. It's always been my habit to get to rehearsals early, feel the stage and what it's like to be in any particular space. My father taught we well, "If you can't be on time, be early."

Years later I was doing an episode of *Cheers* playing opposite Broadway legend Georgia Brown who had introduced the song "As Long As He Needs Me" in *Oliver*. When I walked into the dark empty studio a half hour early, Georgia was sitting at the long table by herself without another soul around. She looked up when she saw me approaching, smiled a huge grin and growled, "Ah! Theatre trained!"

A few minutes after arriving at Town Hall, another of my fellow players arrived. It was the girl playing Bianca and she had brought her three month old son to rehearsal. She was very sweet to me, even though I found out it was her husband I had replaced in the show. She told me that she didn't care because she was going to divorce him anyway citing the fact that she didn't think he was all there. She acknowledged that her husband had talent but that he was troubled.

Her baby was adorable. Still wrinkled and full of baby smell, she told me that she knew her son would grow up to be a great actor. She was rig ht.

As I watched, she carried the infant to center stage and held him up as if offering him to the Gods of The Theatre, like Kunte Kinte in *Roots* being presented to the Universe. "This will be your life, my son" she said, "This will be your life." The little child held his arms out as if to embrace the idea and agree. When the ritual ended, the actress introduced herself to me. Her name was Mary Jo Slater and her son was named Christian. Years later, as I watched Christian Slater star in film after film, I thought of the day his mother held him up and dedicated him to the acting profession.

Among the others in the cast were John Call, a roly-poly little elf of a character actor and his son, Tony Call, who was a longtime star of *One Life To Live*. We were to open the day after Christmas, 1969 for a ten performance run. Although this was only my second professional show, I didn't need to be a seasoned veteran to know that Sid Slon couldn't direct himself out of the men's room. He was a sweet, erudite man who could write and tell a story but didn't know how to block actors on a stage or work with them in any way that they could understand. There were the hugest fights over the littlest things, especially between Sid and Tony Call who was a method actor. After a few days of rehearsals the more experienced actors started to direct the play themselves.

Our opening was preceded by one of the largest snowstorms in the history of New York City. As a result, our first performance at Town Hall, which sat over twelve hundred people was attended by an audience of twenty-five. Sid called it a marvelous opportunity for an extra rehearsal. The show lasted two weeks and during that time, since I was the only one who had not given Sid any grief, I was invited to the Players Club on almost a daily basis.

It was extraordinary for me as a young actor just starting out to rub shoulders with some of the greatest names in the theatre. I would sit at the Players' bar downstairs with Sid Slon and so many ghosts. He said Bert Lahr would walk into the grill.

"How are you today, Bert?" someone would ask.

"Talented," came the reply from the Cowardly Lion, "Talented!"

Sid thought that I should join the Club and I was the first to agree. I needed a sponsor and a second. Sid would sponsor me and Davy Burns was my second. The day came when I had to go before the Board of Directors for an interview. They would decide whether or not I would be admitted. Roland Winters, who made a name playing Charlie Chan in the movies as well as some stereotypical heavies, was the new president of the club having just taken over from Alfred Drake, the great star of *Oklahoma, Kiss Me, Kate* and *Kismet*.

The day came for my interview which was to take place at four p.m. in the fourth-floor board room. Sid thought it would be a good idea if I got there early to hang out and meet some of the other members who could put in a good word for me. I got there just after lunch and went down to the bar where Sid was at a table for four with two other men.

I walked over and recognized one of the men immediately. It was Frank McHugh who was one of

Hollywood's most beloved character actors. He was Bing Crosby's sidekick priest-pal from *Going My Way* and also as the man who had replaced Davy in *Forum*.

Sid made the introductions: "Jim Brochu, I'd like you to meet Frank McHugh."

"Hello, Mr. McHugh. Great to meet you."

"And," continued Sid, "say hello to Jimmy Cagney."

The other man came into focus, my heart stopped and my head pounded and indeed I was shaking the hand of one of my favorite actors of all time, James Cagney. He stood. To meet me? Good Lord! "Have a seat pal," he said sounding just like Jimmy Cagney, "I hear you're up for membership. A little youth is a welcome addition to a bunch of old farts like us."

"Thanks, Mr. Cagney. *Yankee Doodle Dandy* is my favorite film of all time."

Cagney laughed, scrunching his face and said, "Mine too. And call me Jim." Being a bit startled by his openness, I stupidly said, "You can call me Jim, too."

The Membership committee was taking their time and the interviews were going well over their appointed hour. I didn't care. It just gave me more time to spend with one of my idols. After an hour or so of stories it was my turn to face the committee. I went upstairs, passed the library which contained the finest Shakespeare collection outside of the Folger in Washington; along the glass case which displayed George Arliss's costume from *Richelieu* and into the conference room where twelve grim-faced men welcomed me with stony silence.

Roland Winters sat in the middle. Next to him was the past presidents, Alfred Drake and Dennis King, along with Vice President George Melville Cooper; all familiar faces from the stage and screen. Mr. Winters asked me my name, what kind of acting credits I had, what my aspirations were and then the biggie, "Why do you want to be a member of this club?"

Without hesitation I answered, "Any place where a little nobody like me can sit and talk to James Cagney as an equal is a place I want to be a part of." Despite ending the sentence with a preposition, I left the room a Player. Fifty years later, I'm still a proud member.

The Players Club was famous for their Pipe Nights - an occasion, usually of a Sunday evening where the membership would pay tribute to a great star of the stage or screen. They had been after Cagney for years to be an honoree but he was put off by the long head table of speechmakers in tuxedos delivering what he called "eulogies" rather than tributes.

Finally, he relented and agreed to be honored but with a couple of conditions. There would be no speeches. Instead, after dinner Cagney would take to the stage with three friends - Roland Winters, Frank McHugh and Robert Montgomery (Elizabeth's dad). They sat in front of the packed house at a card table and just talked to each other. For three glorious hours. One story after the other. Living history.

I invited my father to be my "date" for the evening and it was the right choice. He found himself in the midst of every star he had ever loved growing up and just to be in Cagney's presence was for him, like myself, a dream come true. It was a marvelous night - filled with stories of Bette Davis, Eddie Rickenbacker, Jack Warner and the old days of Hollywood.

My father and I waited on line to say hello to Cagney and when we made it to the front, Cagney looked at me and said, "Good evening, James! How's our newest member?" I couldn't believe he had remembered my name but that's the kind of man he was. I introduced him to my father. Cagney took his hand, shook it soundly and said, "I know you! I know you from somewhere! How do I know you?" My dad just answered, "I'm from Washington Heights and we're woven of the same cloth, Jimmy." That night brought my father and I closer than any other I could remember.

Aside from the Pipe Nights, the Players would have a "Sunday With The Stars" series. They would honor a movie star with a buffet lunch and then show the star's favorite film. The star would then make a little speech and have a few cocktails before calling it an afternoon.

The first "Sunday with the Stars" I attended was for Bette Davis. I was struck by this giant of the screen being so miniscule. I think she nearly stood five feet but you could hear that laugh of hers across the room. We gathered in the main dining room which had been turned into a little movie theatre to watch the film of her choice. It was *The Catered Affair* with Debbie Reynolds and Ernest Borgnine, the story of a middle class Bronx family whose daughter's wedding was about to split the family apart.

Davis strode into the room to a standing ovation, a drink in one hand and a cigarette in the other. "I guess you're giving me this honor because you think I'm going to die soon. Well, I'm not! But let's have a good time anyway."

Another icon they honored was Gloria Swanson, who could have been even more diminutive than Davis. The film of the day was, of course, *Sunset Boulevard*. Swanson was in New York appearing on Broadway in *Butterflies Are Free*. I found myself in a group with Miss Swanson holding court. She was being very coy and flirty with everyone telling how she found it fabulous to be appearing on Broadway and leaving the stage door to find such loving crowds. After a few weeks, she noticed that those at the stage door were mostly men. Encouraging one of us to ask her, Miss Swanson kept saying "Of course, I can't tell you what I think when I see all those guys waiting for autographs."

"Oh tell us, tell us, tell us. You can tell us what you think," we all implored.

"Well," she said in a stage whisper that included everyone in the room, "just because Judy's dead why do they all flock around me now?"

The phone rang one afternoon in 1973 and it was Joan Crawford. She told me she had been asked by the Players Club to be a "Sunday Afternoon Star" and wanted to know from someone she trusted what the afternoon would be like and should she accept? I told her it would be great. They would have a luncheon, show her favorite film, have a cocktail party and she'd be home by seven. I added that she would have a wonderful time, see a lot of old friends and make some new ones. I knew after knowing her now for some thirteen years that Joan was basically shy but the idea of being the center of attention in a roomful of men for an afternoon appealed to her. She asked if I would be her escort for the day and I happily agreed.

She had moved from the duplex apartment at 2 East 70th Street to a less expensive apartment on East 69th between Park and Lexington after the Board of Directors of Pepsi unceremoniously dumped her a few years before. The Players were sending a car for her, so we met in the lobby of Imperial House and drove down to Gramercy Park together. Like any great star would say as we got out of the limo in front of The Players, "How do I look?"

"Absolutely gorgeous, Joan." I replied. "Absolutely gorgeous!"

She smiled, kissed me on the cheek, said "Bless you" and indicated she was ready to face the troops. A small cadre of fans was waiting for her. I got out first, took her hand and helped her out of the car. She was surrounded at once and patiently signed each and every autograph book before we went in. The welcoming committee stood at the top of the stairs and led the applause as she came up into the great hall and sat on the couch before the fireplace. Without asking, I went to the bar and got her a vodka on the rocks which I placed in front of her as people made their obeisance.

I didn't know until that day that her favorite film was *A Woman's Face* with Melvyn Douglas and Conrad Veidt. I had never seen the film before and knew instantly why she liked it even more than *Mildred Pierce*. She acted up a storm in a very quiet way in a role where the character learned that one could still find love with a horrible facial disfigurement. For Joan, with all her beauty, felt a disfigurement of the soul.

There was only one unpleasant moment for her during the whole afternoon. She got upstaged. While we were sitting on the couch having a conversation with Lester Rawlins, an actor who was on her favorite soap, a burst of applause erupted near the front door. Naturally, all heads turned to see who was coming up the stairs. There appeared one of Joan's arch-enemies who had come to make a guest appearance - Joan Fontaine.

Crawford smiled broadly and even joined in the applause. As the two Joans' eyes met, Fontaine put her arms out and swept over to the couch. Crawford also put her arms out as she rose to embrace her fellow Oscar winner, but under her breath and beneath the smile, I thought I heard her whisper, "The bitch!"

The Player's Club was where I first met Sid Caesar who had the most incredible memory of anyone with whom I ever worked. Caesar was another of my childhood idols. I would glue myself in front of the television every Saturday night to watch *Your Show of Shows* with Caesar, Imogene Coca, Carl Reiner and Howard Morris. There wasn't a great deal of laughter in our house - except on Saturday night. One day I would be one of his writers.

Dad and me on board the Bergensfjord in 1962 on our way to the North Cape of Norway

CHAPTER FIVE
School, Stock and Schwartz

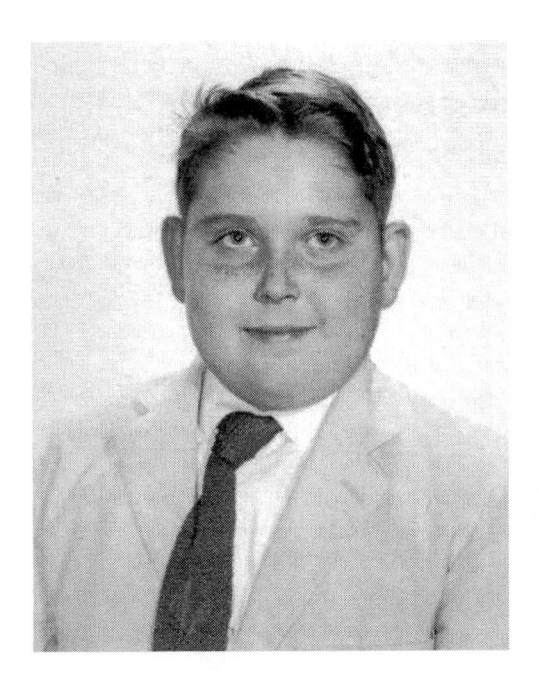

My Official Seventh Grade photo wearing my spiffy O.L.A. tie and long pants.

Of all the treasures my father bestowed on me, the greatest was a first-class education. Of course, every Catholic child was sentenced to eight years of indoctrination in parochial school. My grammar school was Our Lady of Angels at the corner of 74th Street and Fourth Avenue in Bay Ridge, run by the exceptionally misnamed Sisters of Charity. We all wore O.L.A. uniforms – blue jumpers and white blouses for the girls; white shirts, blue and gold ties, black knee socks and navy-blue knickers for the boys. Yes, KNICKERS.

Our class of 40 was co-ed and we were told every morning how lucky we were to have been born Catholic, the one true religion because every other religion guaranteed a one-way, first class ticket to hell. Sister Mary Frances, who had a kind face, scared me with her description of the eternal fires and endless suffering for sinners. So by the time I got home on that first day, I was shaking with the belief that hell would be my fate because of my innate wickedness.

The first class every morning was Catechism, a book of a hundred questions and answers about the faith that we were to commit to memory. One day Sister Frances took the crucifix from over the blackboard and walked up and down the aisles of the class carrying the cross like a cradled baby. She would stop at each desk for a moment so we could get a better look at it and study the contorted agony on Jesus' face. Here comes the blasphemy: I always found the naked figure of Jesus hanging on the cross to be somewhat erotic. Funny how a crucifix can awaken an attraction to the male body.

But when she described the gory details of the crucifixion – the scourging, the beatings, the crown of thorns, the blood and the gore – I felt sick to my stomach. Then, practically in the same breath, she told us that we were the ones responsible for Jesus' torturous end because we were all bad due to original sin and his death was my personal responsibility. In my heart, I didn't buy it for a minute. But when you are hammered with the same message day after day, and then have it reinforced by your family, a six-year old starts to believe it as "gospel" truth.

For months after, I couldn't look at a tomato because it reminded me of blood which reminded me of Jesus' death which reminded me that it was all my fault.

We were taken into the Church to prepare for first communion. Our Lady of Angels Church was a truly breathtaking building. The Roman style, marble-walled church consumed a half-block of the avenue and was truly a beautiful edifice. The ceilings were thirty feet high without a column to obstruct the view. Over the altar was the painting of Our Lady of the Angels by Arturo Murillo and at the north entrance, a full-sized replica of the Pieta.

In second grade we were being prepared to make our first Holy Communion. All of us from the first grade were still together as we moved to another room under the tutelage of Sister Rita, a large monolith in black with a steely granite face. Sister Rita made us believe that receiving the second sacrament of the church, the first being Baptism, would be one of the most profound experiences of our young life because we would be swallowing the body, blood, soul and divinity of Jesus himself. She told us about the great saints who upon receiving communion would levitate, have visions of the risen Christ or find the precious blood pouring out of their mouths. The anticipation was staggering, amplified by her constant reminders that we were not worthy – but we were going to receive him anyway.

We practiced for weeks every day by lining up single file in front of her desk where she would mumble something in Latin and then place an unholy Necco candy wafer on our tongues in lieu of the consecrated unleavened bread. In the days leading up to the big ceremony we practiced in the church and knelt at the altar rail where Sister Rita would deposit the candy on our tongues and we would solemnly process back to our place in the assigned pew.

The night before the ceremony I couldn't sleep because I knew that within hours my life would change and I would feel the presence of God within me, having taken him orally. I was sure I would levitate the second the host hit my tongue. I even put a few band aids in my pocket in case I also received the stigmata. Next morning, I donned the white suit of purity bought especially for the occasion which, with my chubby figure, made me look like a walking igloo.

We made our way to the church where we assembled in our ensembles and began our procession down the main aisle to the blast of the organ.

Entering the church at the beginning of a solemn ceremony was the most thrilling part of Catholicism. The golden altar illuminated by sacred candles, the purple cassocks of the monsignori, the embroidered vestments and the incense that perfumed the whole church with the swing of a thurible. Later in life I would call those things the costumes, the scenery, the make-up, the props.

Our pastor, Bishop Edmund J. Reilly, was the last to enter the church and took his place on the altar, underscoring the momentous event that was about to occur. We were told if the bread stuck to the roof of your mouth, we were forbidden to touch it because, after all, it was the body of Christ. I couldn't understand why it was okay to lick Him but not touch Him.

The moment came for communion and we knelt in a line at the altar rail. As the Bishop approached, I could feel my heart pound as I prepared for take-off. I was about to experience my first transformative religious epiphany. At last he stood in front of me and mumbled, "Corpus Domini Nostrum Jesu Christi" (Body of Christ). I answered, "Amen," closed my eyes and opened my mouth. I felt the wafer touch my tongue and waited for the miracle. And waited. And waited. Nothing. No thrill, no goosebumps, no sudden experience of Jesus. No soaring to the apse. Nothing. In fact, the rehearsal candy had a much greater effect because it at least had a satisfying taste.

I marched back to my seat and dutifully knelt, eyes closed, stooped in a prayerful position (as we had been taught) and continued to wait. I'm still waiting.

After the ceremony, my father treated everyone to dinner at the White Shutter, a special occasion restaurant. The disappointment on my face can be seen in the family photo. If I had been lied to about communion, what else had I been taught was a lie?

I was a pretty good student and loved school. I only got into trouble once when a series of homes was being torn down along the school property to make way for the new school building. In the late 50s, The parish was growing and the old school was bursting at the seams with forty or more boys and girls to a class.

We were forbidden to go near the deconstruction and if we did and were caught, we would be punished with a dose of "The Black Medicine." Just the thought of it sent shivers down my spine. It was the ultimate punishment to be administered; a dose of liquid conspicuously displayed in Mother Superior's office.

My pals Joey Maresca, Emmitt O'Connor, Charlie Brown (for real) and I decided to explore the ruins of the half-demolished homes. Our timing was impeccable, as our exploration began at the same time as the sisters' afternoon constitutional. Mother Superior herself had caught us and ordered us to her office immediately for punishment – a dose of the Black Medicine.

Joey, Emmitt, Charlie and I lined up and one by one she took us into the office and closed the door. Anticipation is always more nerve-wracking than the action itself. When I walked in, the bottle was already on the table along with an extra-large spoon. I stood in front of her as she poured a generous dose. It looked just like the black liquid shoe polish my grandmother used to de-scuff my shoes.

She ordered me to put my head back and open my mouth, the same position in which to receive communion. I felt the spoon touch my bottom lip and then the black viscous goo roll over my tongue and down my throat. My whole body shuddered. I couldn't help but roll my tongue over the roof of my mouth which only caused me to taste it more. I hated the taste of it and then realized what it was. Licorice. A very concentrated licorice syrup. And I HATE licorice. It truly was punishment for me but certainly had more of an effect on me than the consecrated host.

My only other transgression came in the 8th grade when the nuns threatened me with not only physical harm, but the loss of my immortal soul. I had my first truly religious experience in the summer before my last year of grammar school when my father took me to see Ethel Merman in *Gypsy*. It was thrilling and life changing. But the Legion of Decency had condemned the musical and we were forbidden by Pius XII himself to see the production or face the prospect of an eternity in hell. I took my chances.

I ordered a published copy of the musical and when it arrived, I put on the album and then read all the scenes between the songs. I was so excited that I brought the book to school to show my classmates and relive the experience with them. As I was going through the pictures in the book with Joey Maresca, he lingered over a picture of Tessie Tura, Miss Mazeppa and Miss Electra, the three strippers featured in "You Gotta Get A Gimmick."

Before I knew what was happening, I heard a shriek behind me. It was Sister Anthony standing over my shoulder looking at the forbidden book racy photos.

"Where did you get this?" she demanded.

"I sent away for it from the book club, Sister."

"Do you know what this is? It's filth. It's garbage." She steamed.

"No, sister. It's a Broadway musical. And it's really sensational."

"How would you know that?"

"My father took me to see it this summer and I met Ethel Merman after."

"I'll take that!" she said as she grabbed the book out of my hand and put it under her cape. "Tell your father that I wish to see him before class next Monday and I hope you don't get run over by a car and die before confession tomorrow afternoon. Now get in line!"

I didn't see my dad until the next day as he recovered from his Friday night hangover. I braced myself to tell him what had happened. I started crying and he said, "Don't worry about it."

I was thankful I didn't get hit by a car on the way to confession and the priest seemed as nonplussed as my father when I exposed my sin of reading forbidden books to him. I thought the three Hail Marys was a very light sentence for such an egregious crime. My father walked me up to school on Monday and there was Sister Anthony waiting to scold him as she had me.

He walked up to her and said, "I hear you want to talk to me? Well, let's talk."

He guided her by the arm to a more private place of the school yard and all I could see was her face and my father's back. Dad seemed to be doing all the talking and Sister Anthony just stood there listening, her eyes getting wider and her lips growing tighter. She said nothing. After about a minute, he turned and walked back to me and said, "Sister will be returning your book at the end of the day."

Without a word, she told us to form our usual column of twos and she led us silently into the building. At the end of the day, she took the book out of her desk, sans book jacket, and handed it to me without a word, just an icy stare.

Years later, I thought about that incident and asked my father what he had told the nun. He chuckled and said, "I told her if she didn't give you the book back that I would take back my generous contribution to build the new convent. Then I told her I'd buy her two tickets for the show."

There were a lot of changes at home in my last year of grammar school. My Uncle John, my father's younger brother who had been living with us since I was born, decided to get married and move out. He had a very big job at CBS as Operations Manager and found a lovely lady with whom to settle down. They had a child and then, sadly, John died shortly after she was born from a heart attack. He was only forty-two.

Then my grandmother had a slight stroke from which she never fully recovered. So the big question was, where would I go to high school? My first choice was Xaverian High School which was only a few blocks away from home. But my father had the idea that I should go to boarding school and relieve my grandmother from the further stress of raising me.

Several schools were discussed, all of them very ivy league prep. Then my father heard about a place called LaSalle Military Academy which was fifty miles outside of New York City. We went out to look at the place and I was dazzled by the military uniforms, the brass bands, the pomp and circumstance and the attractive cadets. It was run by the Christian Brothers and staffed with former and active army personnel.

So it was decided I go to LaSalle, and thus began three and a half years of living hell. When I arrived to be part of the Class of 1964, my first dormitory room was one I shared with 8 other guys. They were all football jocks and here I was a musical theatre queen at age 13. There was a lot of jumping back and forth between beds that first year, the only thing I really enjoyed.

It was mandatory that young cadets be part of the intramural sports program and I was assigned to a place on the maroon and gray football team. I hated football not only as a spectator but the thought of being a participant was abhorrent.

For our first game, I took my place on the line of scrimmage, opposite an upperclassman who looked me in the eye and snarled, "I'm going to kill you." The play was called, the line moved and I stepped out of his way. I would have handed him the ball if I had it. A few days after this horror on the gridiron, one of the sophomores told me I could be out of the sports program if I joined the Speech and Debate Club. My football sentence was commuted.

I enjoyed all my classes except Math. Any kind of math was out of my reach. It still is. I didn't have the brains for it and in fact, years later, one of my college professors agreed and *passed me* out of the goodness of his heart. My freshman year math teacher was Brother Christopher, an enormous man who stood 6'6" and tipped the scales at three hundred and sixty-five pounds. Naturally his nickname was "Tiny." He had a steely smile that covered a sadistic soul which he allowed to escape from time to time.

Brother Christopher's greatest fury was reserved for those cadets who didn't finish their homework. Punishment would come swiftly and harshly for those who failed. One afternoon, a slacker named Lynch couldn't produce his homework but managed to sputter out a stuttering, unbelievable excuse. Tiny listened patiently, nodding his head as the babbling went on and when Lynch finished, the brother shrugged his shoulders, took a few steps forward and then with a closed fist, turned back and struck Lynch in the head, knocking him out of his chair and across the room. Brother Christopher just smiled and quietly said, "You better do your homework."

La Salle and I were not a good fit. The school was populated by young men who were attracted to the military, contact sports and all sorts of manly activities. I was an artist in the midst of a battlefield. I was definitely an outcast and somewhat bullied although I was never subjected to any beatings, just standoffishness, being called a queer and subjected to ridicule for my lack of any physical prowess.

Then came the Freshman Talent Show where I sang Henry Higgins opening song from *My Fair Lady*, "Why Can't The English?" It turned the tide for me when some of the guys came up and told me, "Gee, you were good. Are you from England?" Appearing in the school plays is what really saved my sanity for those last three years. Brother Eugene, a young, cocky, red-headed Irishman, was the director of the shows and there was a little theater in The Boathouse on the Great South Bay which sat about three hundred uncomfortably.

Once a year we would put on the school play, usually some comedy from the 1920s, and by the second-year, Brother Eugene was picking out the shows for me to play the lead. All of a sudden, I was a star in the school and that recognition of talent ended the derision and made the whole thing bearable. I still despised the marches and the guns and the shooting and the field exercises, even though I earned a chest full of marksman metals.

My father literally bribed me to stay in school. He offered wonderful trips every summer to entice me into one more year. It was worth the devil's bargain to see the world and yet go back to a place I truly hated.

In 2014, I got an invitation from our alumni society to attend our 50th anniversary reunion. The committee wrote that I was the most famous person in our class and they would like to fly me down to Boca Raton to be the special guest of honor. I wrote back saying that I hated my four years there and I never wanted to see any of them ever again. At first they thought I was kidding. I was not. But when I was in Florida doing *Zero Hour*, six classmates and their wives came to see the show and we had our own lovely reunion. They had all become very successful professional men, married fathers and pillars of their communities.

My father wasn't happy with my choice of college. During my last year of grammar school, I had met an actor named Matt Tobin when he appeared at our neighborhood theatre in the production of *The Hasty Heart*. I remembered he had told me he had gone to Carnegie Tech because the drama program was so good there. I also remembered reading that Jack Klugman also went to Carnegie Tech. I thought that's the place for me.

I had to submit all my academic credentials as well as perform an audition in front of Earle Gister, the head of the Drama Department. I passed the audition and was accepted into the Class of 1968. That summer before I went away to Pittsburgh, I studied at the American Academy of Dramatic Arts. It was a wonderful three-month course at the new building which is on Madison and 30th Street focusing on scene study, movement, fencing, singing and character development. I had memorable teachers like Jorie Wyler, an acting coach who told me that I wasn't living up to my potential because I was too lazy. She was absolutely right.

When I arrived in Pittsburgh to begin classes at Carnegie Tech, the first person I met was a fellow New Yorker who was about eighteen months younger than myself and there on a music scholarship. He was a dazzling piano player and a very sweet guy. We became instant friends. He had a talent for music the likes of which I had never seen. We would go to the little music rehearsal rooms in the Fine Arts building and I would mention the name of the song. He would play it from memory and I would sing my lungs out.

His name was Stephen Schwartz who went on to be one of the great composers of the American Musical Theatre.

We started class in September of 1964 and were both excited about the upcoming opening of a new show called *Fiddler On The Roof* based on the stories of Sholem Aleichem.

I told him I knew Zero, and Stephen said he knew Maria Karnilova, who was Zero's co-star playing Golde. We decided to fly home for the weekend to see the second performance of the show. My father had connections with a ticket brokerage firm and so he arranged for us to have seats. When we arrived at the Imperial Theatre, there was only one ticket. Stephen was pissed, as he rightfully should have been and I ran up the street to the broker's office to see if he could get another ticket to what had become the biggest smash of the season. It looked impossible but sure enough, he pulled a rabbit out of the hat – or should I say a ticket out of the box office. The ticket locations were A104 and S22. Steve said he deserved the first row for going through all the angst of not knowing if he could get in. I said to him, "No, you have to sit in S because Schwartz starts with S and Brochu starts with B which is closer to A."

Fiddler was perfect. It, like the lyrics of "Sunrise, Sunset" say, was "laden with happiness and tears." As Zero came out for his call, the theatre rose to its feet as one with screams and bravos like I had never heard before.

As I jumped out of my seat, I caught Zero's eye. He bowed and gave me a little wave, making me feel at one with the universe. After the show I was able to take Stephen backstage and introduce him to Zero, who was transcendent in the part. Absolutely unforgettable. After a few niceties, Stephen brought me upstairs to introduce me to Maria Karnilova.

He had been dating her daughter Katie for a while and they were neighbors on Long Island. I had seen Karnilova in *Gypsy* and was wild to meet Tessie Tura in person.

After the show, we joined my dad at Toots Shor's. Dad asked Stephen if he was an actor too? He said he was a composer-lyricist and his goal was to have two shows running on Broadway at the same time. He went on to have three, win the Oscar, the Tony, the Emmy and the Grammy. Fifty years later we are still friends.

I went to Carnegie Tech for only one year because I didn't feel I was learning anything I didn't already know. I kept getting thrown out of acting classes because I thought the exercises were dumb and I already knew how to enter and exit a stage.

In one class we were given a rolled-up towel and told it was a puppy. We were to hand it around the room and react as we would to a fluffy, cuddly little dog. When it got to me, I passed it to the next student without reacting. The teacher stopped, annoyed, and asked what I was doing? Why hadn't I reacted to the puppy? I told him I was allergic to dogs – and was shown the door.

My father was very happy with my decision to leave Tech and get a more rounded education. My grandmother died during my high school years so I wanted to go to college locally and live back at home. A lot of friends were studying at St. Francis College in Brooklyn Heights and so I decided to complete my degree there.

My three years at St. Francis were a total joy. I dove into all the activities and became Editor-In-Chief of the school newspaper and president of the Troupers, the college drama society. Dad was thrilled when I made *Who's Who In American Colleges and Universities*. Between my junior and senior year, I read in *Variety* that the American Place Theatre was looking for unusual types for their production of *Endicott and the Red Cross* by Robert Lowell. The Off-Broadway production was to feature British star Kenneth Haigh who had made a big splash in *Look Back In Anger* in London and be directed by John Hancock who had recently directed a major hit of a movie, *Bang The Drum Slowly*.

I was a big guy, six-feet four and three hundred pounds and a great dancer. Hancock thought I was a good type and so I was cast as Soldier #3 and Indian #4.

The cast was first rate, populated with actors that I had long admired like Ralph Clanton, John Harkins, Leon B. Stevens and Marshall Ephron. Rounding out the cast was a young actor named Spaulding Grey. Spaulding was a rather timid fellow offstage who later achieved international fame with his autobiographical monologues, *Swimming to Cambodia* and *Monster In A Box*.

We gathered for the first rehearsal on the stage of the Theatre at St. Clement's on West 46th Street. After we introduced ourselves, Wynn Handman the producer, introduced us to the playwright, Robert Lowell, a Poet Laureate of the United States.

Lowell welcomed everyone and then told us he would read the play to us to expose the sense of the piece. This was my first professional show and I thought all playwrights read the play to the cast at the first rehearsal. Lowell began in a nasally Boston accent and would stop after every few paragraphs to explain, "Now in these beautifully written lines what I was trying to convey is…" or "In this wonderfully constructed sentence, the meaning…." Not only was he reading the play to us, he was reviewing it as he went along. The play ran ninety minutes, the first reading lasted over four hours. It was the most headache inducing rehearsal I ever worked through. John Hancock was a "realist" director and since a lot of the play took place outside, he thought it would be a good idea to run some of the scenes in Central Park. It was hard to work because it was freezing and we couldn't say the lines through chattering teeth. Lowell was an odd man, sometimes brooding, sometimes engaged, but always with a far-away look in his eyes. Later I found that he was a manic-depressive who spent several stretches in a mental hospital. About ten years after *Endicott*, Lowell died of a heart attack in the back of a New York city cab.

Almost fifty years later I would return to the stage of St. Clement's as Zero Mostel in *Zero Hour*, a long journey from my unforgettable performance as Soldier #3.

Robert Lowell discusses the play with Kenneth Haigh during our Central Park rehearsal. Below is me on the left wearing a tin can as Soldier #3

In my last year at St Francis, one of my assignments as the head of the Drama Society was to produce theatrical special events. I thought a fun and enlightening wonderful afternoon would be to have David Burns and Kate Reid come out and talk to the students about their work on Broadway and especially *The Price,* in which they were both appearing.

Kate asked me, "What time?"

I said, "Eleven a.m."

She said, "That's when I'm going to bed." I told her we'd send a car for her and that it would be fun, so she agreed. When the day of their appearance came, she was totally hung over and didn't want to do it, but she also felt she had made a commitment and didn't want to disappoint me or the students. She put on a pair of dark glasses, made sure she was allowed to smoke, once there, and we all went to Brooklyn where Davy and Kate held forth in one of the funniest hours I've ever spent. Davy, as usual, took nothing seriously and answered every straight forward question with a joke. I was the moderator, but of course, couldn't get a word in. At one point, a photographer came down the aisle and started to take some pictures. Davy looked at the photographer and said, "Stop! Brochu and I have lived together as man and wife in Budapest and have never been photographed together!" I thought Kate Reid was going to fall out of her chair. She howled and the photo was snapped.

In the early seventies an actor could make good and easy money by winning on game shows. The rules for being a contestant were far less strict than they are now and you could do as many game shows as you could get on. Today the rules say you can do no more than one a year, not that there are that many major network game shows anymore.

I have been a game show fan since I was a kid. I loved the sophistication of Arlene Francis and Bennett Cerf on *What's My Line?* and loved playing along with Kitty Carlisle and Peggy Cass on *To Tell The Truth*. I saw an ad in the paper that they were looking for contestants for *The $10,000 Pyramid*, one of my favorite shows, and decided to try out.

The contestant coordinator, who would decide if you got on the show, was named Edy Chan. I walked into her office expecting to see a little Chinese lady but instead, Edy Chan was a red-headed, roly-poly, jolly brick of a woman who was more Irish than the Blarney Stone.

I played a sample game with her and she put me on the show. Dick Clark was the host and my partner was Adrienne Barbeau. I was on the last show of five shows taped that day and Miss Barbeau was exhausted. It was an embarrassing loss and I left the studio heartsick.

A few months later, Edy Chan called me and asked if I was interested in being on a new game show called *Three On a Match*. Sure! Bill Cullen hosted the show and I was shocked when he walked onto the stage with the most pronounced limp I had ever seen in my life. And yet, the camera never shot him below the waist so the home audience never knew.

I won a trip to Acapulco on *Three On A Match* and then Edy put me on Jackpot! where I won a Chevy Nova and $5.000. In 1970, that was big money. But then the FCC made it much harder to be a contestant and so my next game show was in the early nineties – a second place finish on *Jeopardy*! Winning a recliner and year's supply of Reese's' Marshmallow Cups. I made my last game show appearance in 2012 when I made a nice piece of change on *Who Wants To Be A Millionaire?* hosted by Meredith Vieira, the classiest lady on television.

I was about to go for the really big money but stepped away on a playwright question because I didn't want to take a chance. I would have lost what I had and as Grandma Minnie would say, "A bird in the hand…" But I knew the answer and am still kicking myself years later for not going for it. A few weeks later, I got a handwritten note from Meredith thanking me for being such a fun contestant. Now that's class.

The Goodspeed Opera House is an absolute jewel of a theatre that sits on the banks of the Connecticut River.

It was built in 1876 and was a revival house for the great musicals of the 20s and 30s, as well as a testing ground for future Broadway hits. Both *Annie* and *Man of La Mancha* started there. I was hired to do three shows that first year: *Good News* with my old pal Mary Jo Catlett, *Sunny* starring Leland Palmer and *Where's Charley?* with the rubber-faced Bill McCutcheon in the lead.

I was invited back the next season for two shows: George M. *Cohan's Forty-five Minutes from Broadway* and then to play an eighty-year-old gardener in a new musical, *Something's Afoot*. I had done a year's worth of backers' auditions for *Afoot* which was getting its second production at Goodspeed. The show finally made it to Broadway ten years later but lasted only a few performances.

In 1970, my friend Jeanne Arnold was appearing in the musical *Coco*, starring Katharine Hepburn. She invited me to see the show and then meet the great lady after the performance. Hepburn was extraordinary the night I saw her, despite her having a nosebleed that poured through most of the first act.

After the show, I was escorted backstage and found myself standing in front of Hepburn's dressing room next to Steve Lawrence and Eydie Gorme. The stage manager knocked on Hepburn's door. It opened a crack. I could see the famous cheekbones and the turned-down lips and a bit of eye staring out suspiciously through the small opening. The stage manager said, "Miss Hepburn, would you say hello to Steve and Eydie?"

Hepburn opened the door wide, barked, "Hello Steve and Eydie," and closed the door before they said a word. The stage manager shrugged and led the famous couple back from whence they came. I thought if they got that kind of reception, what am I going to get?

Jeanne knocked again. "Kate, it's Jeannie!" Hepburn opened the door wide and said, "So sorry about the bloody nose. Thanks for the hanky. This must be your friend."

"Hello, Miss Hepburn, you were…"

"Call me Kate! Sorry you had to see the show tonight with my gusher."

"I didn't notice anything except a brilliant performance."

She laughed and introduced me to her companion, Phyllis Weyburn, who was sitting quietly in the corner. Hepburn asked Jeanne if she was going to go to George Rose's apartment for ice cream. Jeanne said she'd love to and Kate invited me as well. "I'm sure George won't mind, and the more the merrier."

I actually had gotten to know George during the run of *The Canterbury Tales*, so I didn't feel shy about going. As our little entourage left the Mark Hellinger, there was a large group of fans waiting for autographs (which she never gave) or just a glimpse. A few steps from Hepburn's car, a girl of about fourteen jumped out in front of her and with an air of desperation said, "Miss Hepburn, you've given me the will to go on." Hepburn brushed past her and said, "Well if I've given you the will to go on, you ought to go out and stick your head in a pond." And jumped into the car.

A few months later at Goodspeed, as we were about to begin a performance of *Something's Afoot*, I heard a commotion in the audience. It was Hepburn making an entrance and getting wild applause. She sat in the fifth-row center with her knees buckled up on the seat in front of her. At the intermission the stage manager came back and said, "Katharine Hepburn is here."

"I know. Everybody knows."

"She would like to come back after the show and see you and Mary Jo." Well, the cast looked as if they had been hit in the face with a pie. Sure enough, after the show, Hepburn made her way down the hall looking at me and when she got about five feet away, said with a twinkle, "Do you remember me?"

I said, "You do look somewhat familiar."

She couldn't have been more effusive about the show and greeted all the cast members warmly. She said she had been up very early and thought she'd be sound asleep by now but the show was so entertaining and we had kept her awake. High praise indeed. She asked if Mary Jo Catlett and I like to come back to her house, Fenwick, and share some blueberry bread that she had made that afternoon? She said it was a hard place to find, so we were to leave our cars at the theatre and her brother Dick would drive us down. Hepburn went on ahead and when we arrived at the property, Dick barreled through the gate, featuring a hand-made sign that read, *Please Go Away!* Kate was at the door waiting for us. She escorted us down the hallway where it looked like a rummage sale from a sporting goods store. Tennis rackets, golf clubs, nets, baseball bats, croquet mallets and every kind of game equipment littered the entrance.

She led us into the living room and despite the fact that it was a sweltering August night, there was a roaring fire in the fireplace. She loved a fire in the hearth more than anything.

As she was showing us around the house, I couldn't help but think about all the famous visitors that had seen these walls – Spencer Tracy, Howard Hughes, Cary Grant, governors, presidents – and now, me.

She took us into the kitchen where the homemade blueberry bread was waiting for us on the counter. When Kate said, "Come for blueberry bread," that's what she meant, for not even a glass of water was offered to go with it.

I didn't see Hepburn again after that night but we continued a happy correspondence for years. She invited me to visit her in New York but the timing never worked out. I would write her long newsy letters and get short, but very sweet, notes in return.

Many years later, I became friends with Katharine Houghton, Kate's niece, and co-star in *Guess Who's Coming To Dinner*. She would keep me informed of her aunt's declining health and told me that Kate's end was a sad one. Because she was on oxygen, the only thing that gave her true joy had to be taken away. A roaring fireplace. Even in the sultry heat of an August evening.

A week after I left Goodspeed I was cast in the Manhattan Theatre Club production of *Berkeley Square*, a time-travel play by John Balderston, based on a Henry James novella. It's the story of Peter Standish, a young man who rents a flat in London's Berkeley Square and is magically transported back to the late 18th Century. I was totally miscast as King George III but the part was small and the cast was great fun.

The role of Peter Standish went to a young unknown actor named Christopher Reeve who was so stunningly handsome he took my breath away. I had the misfortune of sharing a dressing room with him. I say misfortune because he used to run around only in his jockey shorts and I was in a constant state of tumescence. I used to drive him home in my VW bug after the show and did everything in my power not to make a pass at him.

Our friendship didn't end well because I got bored on stage and misbehaved as badly as Zero, trying to break up the other actors. Chris got angry at me because I wasn't taking my profession seriously. Our warm friendship turned icy and I didn't see Chris for thirty years until I was asked to write and direct a benefit for his foundation.

When I heard about his horrible accident, I, like everyone, felt terrible so when I got the job I was hoping it would be a time to heal. When his wife Dana wheeled Christopher in, he looked at me and smiled that dazzling smile. I knelt down in front of him, put my hand on top of his and openly wept telling him how sorry I was for being such a putz so long ago. He looked at me with those super-blue eyes and said, "You may not feel it, but I'm hugging you right now."

Sadly, Chris passed away not long after that evening, followed by his darling wife Dana a year later; a non-smoker who died at the age of forty-four from lung cancer. A few years ago I had the honor of introducing their son Matt Reeve at the Born For Broadway Benefit which continues to raise money for the Chris and Dana Reeve Foundation. He was as much of a Superman off-screen as he was on.

A very healing moment with Chris Reeve.

With Meredith Vieira, the classiest lady on TV.

CHAPTER SIX
Dollys and Orange Drinks

Carol Channing and myself at the tenth Anniversary Reunion party for *Dolly*. She signed the picture twenty-five years later

After making it through the four years of high school spent in the Gulag that was La Salle, I was ready to immerse myself in the world of theatre before I had to report to Carnegie Tech to begin college courses. I had enrolled in an intensive acting course at the American

Academy of Dramatic Arts which was moving into its new home at Madison Avenue and 30th Street.

I was in heaven going from class to class – scene study, fencing, movement, acting – and loved working on scenes (Salinger's *Franny and Zooey* was my biggie).

Our graduation speaker was the distinguished actor and playwright Emlyn Williams, author of *The Corn Is Green*. The class idiot lived up to his name when he announced that Emlyn Williams was his favorite star and he couldn't wait to meet her.

We were all evaluated at the end of the summer. It seems my teachers agreed that I had talent but only did the minimum to get by. Hmmm, the story of my life.

The main bulletin board at the Academy was always peppered with odd job offerings for the students to make some pocket money. One job looked fascinating....only four hours a day, good pay and it was at the old Metropolitan Opera House on 39th Street. The job description was "Bucket Boy" and I would be required to work with the scenic artists high above the stage, cleaning the brushes and emptying buckets. Also I would be required to fetch coffee for the artists. Sounded easy, right? It was the worst two weeks of my life.

I arrived for my first day and walked through the stage door on West 39th Street. The aroma of that musty old house was intoxication personified, a blend of makeup scenery and history.

The doorman told me I was to report to Valodja, the head painter in the paint loft, and he would tell me what to do. Then with an ominous smile he added, "Good luck."

I took what seemed to be the very first elevator ever invented to the top floor and was "greeted" by a wild-eyed Russian who had obviously enjoyed a Danish and vodka for breakfast.

"Who the fuck are you?" he roared.

"I'm the new bucket boy."

He continued in a thick Russian accent, "After you clean those buckets you go for coffee, then you come back and clean the buckets and then do the same at the warehouse. And don't talk to me ever."

I knew on the first day I was not going to last. I might have survived Valodja but there were four others just like him. They were mean, loud and preternaturally rude. But when I came back the second day, I brought my own lunch and sat in the house while Leontyne Price performed the dress rehearsal of *Aida*. Yes, the job did have its perks like using the stage door and being able to explore all the different areas of the house.

On the third day, I came to work to find the stage was set for *Madame Butterfly*. All the lights were on but the stage was empty. No singers or stagehands. The curtain was down and it was absolutely quiet. I cautiously walked onto the stage, looking around. As I got to stage center, I closed my eyes and pretended I was singing on the stage of the great Met. About a second later, the grand drape parted and I looked down to see the conductor and full orchestra about to do a music run through. Exit, stage right!

Working in the paint loft, you could hear the music rising skyward, only to be punctuated by the screams of the Mad Russian. His screams were usually directed at me for any minor infraction of his arbitrary rules. The end came after he almost hit me for bringing the wrong coffee order. But the joy of the job was working at the building itself whose walls vibrated with the sounds of singing ghosts. Watching rehearsals with Birgit Nilsson as Salome or Anna Moffo as Cho-Cho San was unforgettable. It's a shame that jewel of a theatre was torn down.

My other part time job was working the concessions at the back of Broadway Theatres. The job paid $18.00 a week but once again I got to go through the stage door. I told my father that I had taken the job and he hit the ceiling. He was worried about me taking the long subway ride back to Bay Ridge at midnight. But I put my foot down. I was almost eighteen and could take care of myself.

The first night on the job was at *A Funny Thing Happened on the Way to the Forum.*

I was actually working at the Alvin Theatre and almost felt a part of the cast. On my first night there, the show broke a little after eleven p.m. and I started to worry that my father was right. I was a little apprehensive about the long train ride at that hour.

I walked out of the theatre among the exiting crowd to find Buddy Wallace and his limo waiting for me in front. Dad had sent him to drive me home. I still enjoyed thinking about the looks on the patrons' faces as they gaped at the $18.00 a week orange drink boy climb into his waiting limo and drive off.

The summer of '64, I asked the Golub Brothers, my bosses who owned all the Broadway concessions, if they would station me at the St. James Theatre where *Hello, Dolly!* was playing so I could hang out with Davy, who was playing Horace Vandergelder. God, he and Channing were a magical couple together. His Vandergelder was gruff and adorable and when he and Channing danced at the end of the show, there wasn't a dry eye in the house. Davy gave me this picture of himself as Vandergelder, one of my most treasured memories. It says, "To my pal Jim, Until death do we part. Davy Burns."

I spent seven years (on and off) behind the concession stand during the run of *Hello, Dolly!* and I may be the only man still around who saw all seven Dollys and the understudy, Bibi Osterwald. I even watched Channing's original understudy rehearse the part, a lady named JoAnne Worley.

Each Dolly was unique in her own way. Ginger Rogers was cute, Martha Raye was funny, Pearl Bailey was charismatic, Betty Grable was vixinish, Phyllis Diller proved to be a passionate Dolly, Bibi Osterwald (the understudy) played her like an Irish washwoman and Merman…well, Merman was Merman. But Channing was the best. Her performance was almost profound.

Davy asked me if I wanted to come to the dress rehearsal for Martha Raye who was going into the show that night. Martha made her entrance, jumped off the trolley, forgot her first line and to cover she reached into the enormous handbag she carried, looked in and said, "Oh, what's here? Looks like a Mehron 28A and a dildo!" There were only ten of us sitting in the audience but we all rolled out of our chairs. Even Mr. Merrick.

I had a lot of friends in the cast and being able to hang out backstage, I got to know each Dolly, some more than others but more than a nodding acquaintance. Carol, Ginger, Martha, Betty, Phyllis and Ethel were all very nice. As you can tell by the story when she encountered a young boy at Sardi's, Pearl was not.

I got to know Channing the best.

With Martha "Maggie" Raye in her dressing room at the St. James. A sweet, funny lady who loved taking her dentures out for a joke.

She seemed almost otherworldly at times: overly-designed, over-sized, wide-eyed automated Kewpie doll. I hadn't seen her in years but we re-connected in 1997 to mixed results.

We were becoming close friends. She was living in Palm Springs with her cousin Richard Long. I went down to help her organize her book. When I got there, she had pages and chapters all over her bedroom. Nothing was together. I can still hear her saying in her most Channing-esque delivery, "Jim dear, would you see if Ethel Merman is on the bed?"

Her cousin Richard's third wife, a Filipino lady who married a wealthy older man, took an immediate dislike to me. I could tell she didn't like that Carol had someone in her life that wasn't her. Can anyone say control freak?

In 1998, Steve and I were nominated for an L.A. Stage Ovation Award, the Los Angeles equivalent of Broadway's Tony. It was going to be a star studded event and the producers asked me if I would ask Carol to present the Award for Best Musical, which was coincidentally the category for which Steve and I had been nominated. They would send a car for her and treat her like royalty. She accepted and asked if she could bring Dickie's wife. It would be nice for her to have company for the long ride. Of course. Whatever she wanted.

Carol arrived for the ceremony out of sorts because the ride was longer than expected and Dickie's wife complained all the way. But everything was on track for a great evening.

Carol and I at the beginning of the Ovation Awards. We wouldn't be smiling by the end of the evening.

The producer explained to Carol that she had to give out two awards: Best Musical in a Small Theatre and Best Musical in a Large Theatre. Steve and I were up for Musical in a Large Theatre. Carol said she

Carol and Charles reuniting after thirty years

understood and we joined the great atmosphere with all the celebs in the green room. Dickie's wife said she could make better guacamole.

The only tense moment was when Charles Nelson Reilly entered. Charles played Cornelius Hackl in the original *Dolly* production and he and Carol didn't exactly leave on the best terms. Charles thought Carol had some cast members fired. He was still angry thirty years later. Charles was a friend. I spoke to him before the show and told him Channing would be there and begged him to make up. After all that time, to let bygones be bygones. When Charles walked into the party, he spotted Steve and I sitting with Channing and made a beeline over to us. I crossed my fingers and hoped there wouldn't be a scene. Charles couldn't have been more charming to her. He even brought her a flower.

I was sitting with Steve in the fifth row when Carol was announced and the crowd rose as one in a roar. She announced the winner of the Small Theatre and she was confused. She thought Steve and I had lost since someone else accepted. She stopped the proceedings and said, "And now I'd like to give my own Diamond Award to Steve Schalchlin and Jim Brochu for *The Last Session*." We shrank down in our chairs. She was stopping the show to give us two plastic diamond rings. I went to the foot of the stage (Steve just slumped down farther in his seat) and took the rings. I didn't want to go up because it wasn't the Ovation and I thought it would be disrespectful. I took the rings and waived to the crowd and then I saw Channing trying to exit. I yelled at her, "Carol, you have to give another award."

"What?" she yelled back.

"You have to give another award!"

Steve and I showing off our Diamond Awards

She turned and saw the young man holding the envelope with the name of the winner and shrugged. The audience went wild. When they calmed down, she came back to the mic, like the true star she was and growled, "It's a little like exiting into a closet, isn't it?"

When I met her in the lobby, I asked if she wanted to stay for the party. She thought it was a great idea since she was having a wonderful time. Dickie's wife was not. I told her to stay exactly where she was because I had to seriously go to the bathroom and I would be right back to escort her into the affair.

I walked about five steps when one of the theatre doors opened and Bea Arthur burst through, a woman on a mission. She saw me and said, "Thank God. Jimmy, do you have any money?" Before I could answer she took my arm and led me to the bar. "I don't have any money. Buy me a drink, will you. Grey Goose on the rocks."

I said, "But Bea, I got Channing over there."

"Fuck her!" came the reply. "It will only take a minute."

I took Bea to the bar, ran to the men's room and then ran back to get Channing. She was gone. I asked around and somebody told me she had left. I didn't make much of it until the next day when the phone rang at 7:30 a.m. It was Carol. "You abandoned me!"

I asked her what she was talking about. She told me that Dickie's wife had told her that I had left her standing there and ran off with Bea Arthur. She assured Carol I wasn't coming back.

I got angry and told her it was she who abandoned me and that Dickie's wife had lied to her. True, I had taken Bea to the bar but I was back in three minutes to take her to the party. Dickie's wife was determined to put a wedge between us and she succeeded. And we didn't win that night either.

But soon after, Carol married her childhood sweetheart and found love at last. About two years after our incident, I went down to the L.A. piers to see them off on the *Crystal Serenity*, a ship I worked on many times and knew all the crew. Carol asked me if I could get her an officers' uniform to wear during the cruise. She never took it off for the whole two weeks.

I saw Carol for the last time in 2014 while I was doing a benefit at the McCallum Theatre in Palm Springs. She was very weak. She seemed out of it. She didn't remember me.

But in 1964, she was a force of nature giving 100% eight times a week. She was always running past me as I walked up the flight of stairs to Davy's second floor dressing room at the St. James. Dolly was the biggest hit in New York that sweltering summer and I found a second home in that second floor dressing room.

I would tuck myself into my little place on the sofa next to the small bathroom and wait to see who came through to offer their congratulations. I would not have to wait long. In came Gene Kelly and Dan Dailey (his co-stars from *It's Always Fair Weather*), Danny Kaye, Tallulah Bankhead, Mary Martin as well as a bevy of British stars Davy worked with during his London career in the 1930s. Davy always introduced me as "Meet my pal, Jim…" Two frequent heroes of mine dropped by so often that we became great friends – Jack Albertson and Hans Conreid.

The Kentucky Fried Chicken franchise was relatively new in 1964 so for publicity, Colonel Harlan B. Sanders himself would bring buckets of chicken to all the different Broadway theatres after the show and get pictures of himself eating chicken with the stars. I arrived at Davy's dressing room after a Wednesday matinee and found the photographer taking pictures of Colonel Sanders sitting in my little place in the corner of the sofa. Next to him was Sir Noel Coward. They were both munching on chicken legs. Davy offered, "Don't forget, Noel, you met a real Tennessee Colonel tonight!" Without missing a beat or dropping his chicken leg, the Colonel roared, "Kentucky, sir. Kentucky!"

I hope Sir Noel thought it was finger licking good.

An autograph from Ginger, a very sweet lady.

CHAPTER SEVEN
The Good, the Bad and Yvonne DeCarlo

Anything Goes at Surflight.

The Goodspeed Opera House was the Gold Standard of Summer Stock but working in a dump of a theatre in 1969 was the greatest summer of my life. I was doing what I loved and loved what I was doing. I landed a job as the lead character actor at the Surflight Summer Theatre in Beach Haven, New Jersey. The place was run by a fellow named Joe Hayes, a former Broadway chorus boy who made the Energizer Bunny look like a sloth. He was built like a fireplug: short, stocky, crew cut and coke bottle eyeglasses. He hit upon a great system to make a very lucrative living. When his wildly successful Surflight was not running in the summer, Joe was directing revues at local high schools.

He made a deal with each school that he would receive fifty percent of the ticket sales and then would cast two hundred kids in the show. He counted on the fact that each student would bring their two parents and four grandparents, selling at least six tickets per family. When you multiply that by the number of students and the number of high schools plus the income from the always-sold-out Surflight, Joe was making a fortune.

I met Joe Hayes in Davy's dressing room at the 46th Street Theatre when he was doing *The Price* shortly after it transferred from the Morosco where it opened. Davy had just come back to the show when it made the transfer.

Kate Reid stayed with the show but Pat Hingle and Arthur Kennedy left and were replaced by Albert Salmi as the cop and Shepperd Strudwick as the doctor. One afternoon after a matinee I caught the four of them clowning around in Davy's dressing room and snapped off this Polaroid.

Joe came backstage after seeing the show with four Xaverian Brothers who came from a Brooklyn High School. Joe said he was excited to start the new Surflight Summer Season – he was producing twelve musicals in twelve weeks. The cast would perform at night and rehearse the next week's show during the day. Auditions for the season were going to be held the next Friday.

Davy said, "Hire Jim. He's very good."

Joe told me to come with a picture and resume and eight bars of an up tune. David and I were anxious to get out to go to dinner and so he shooed the five of them out of the room. One of the Brothers asked if he could see the stage. Davy said sure and led the way. We headed for the stage door, Joe and the Brothers walked through the other door to the stage.

The 46th Street Theatre was a musical house but the orchestra pit was covered with black velour *when The Price* played there. Just as my hand touched the stage door, we heard a scream in a thud. Obviously one of them fell into the covered pit. Davy just said, "Keep on walking."

When I went to the audition for Surflight, the room was packed with hundreds of aspiring college thespians who wanted the coveted jobs. There would be twenty in the company – six dancers and fourteen principals.

Joe Hayes sat by himself at a desk and made each actor take a number. We all had to watch each other audition and it was absolutely painful. Joe would cut people off after a few notes and say, "Thank you. It will not be necessary for you to stay."

Finally after about an hour my turn came and I started my song, "I'll Never Say No" from *The Unsinkable Molly Brown*. I got to the word "No" and Joe cut me off. But instead of "Thanks and goodbye," he told me to come to the callbacks later that afternoon.

When I came to the call back at 5:30 he had me read a few lines from *The Music Man* and when I finished, he hired me on the spot. I couldn't have been more thrilled.

The pay was a whopping $25.00 a week plus laundry money, room and board.

As I drove down the New Jersey Turnpike on my way to Surflight, I kept imagining what the theater would look like. I pictured a quaint seaside .with plush velvet seats, a red brocade curtain and a golden proscenium.

Surflight was located on Long Beach Island in New Jersey, which was one of the most beautiful pristine beach communities on the coast. When I got to the theater my heart dropped. Instead of the beautiful temple I thought I was going to see, I looked at a converted garage that looked like it was about to fall down. When I went inside, Joe was standing there and he greeted me warmly. "Let's have a look around."

The space was actually an old garage which had been converted into a three hundred seat thrust stage theatre. The plush seating was rusty old folding chairs with pathetic pillows covering them. The stage was the size of a postage stamp and I couldn't imagine having 20 people running around it.

Joe was directing *The Music Man* and he wasn't wasting time. We dove right in. The twenty of us loved each other from the beginning – some more talented than others but not a bad apple in the bunch. I called Davy and told him how it was going then I foolishly invited him to come down for opening night knowing that he would say no. But he said yes.

The day of the opening I had to go up to Stroudsburg, Pennsylvania, pick him up and bring him down to the shore for the show. He sat in the front row. I couldn't believe my eyes that I was playing Mayor Shinn in front of the man who originated the character and won a Tony Award for it.

Joe was very religious and so he had a custom of having a priest bless the theater at the opening of each season. After the priest blessed the theater, Joe announced that he was very proud to have David Burns in the audience and asked him to come up and say a few words.

David rose, walked to the stage, took Joe by the shoulder and said, "Well Joe, I'm delighted to say that you're presenting *The Music Man* tonight the way it was originally intended to be performed - in the nude!" Joe laughed his maniacal laugh and almost pushed Davy back into his seat.

The 1969 Surflight production of *The Music Man* with Davy Burns sitting in the front row. I'm playing Mayor Shinn, the tall one with the top hat, doing a shameless impersonation of him. That's me in the middle wearing the top hat.

Surflight was an idyllic place. It was two blocks from the Ocean and three blocks from the Bay. We were a cast of twenty young people, I being the oldest at the ripe old age of twenty-two. But we were passionate about what we were doing and we all loved each other to a degree I had never encountered with any other cast. 50 years later some of us are still in touch.

After playing Mayor Shinn, I tackled a variety of roles that summer I would never, ever play in my life including a Chinese grandfather and a German valet. But each show was sold out with season ticket holders and after the show we would form a receiving line. The audience would file past us gushing over our performances .A lot of them became friends and would take us on their boats or invite us to their houses to sit by the pool. When we were doing Anything Goes, the leading lady was a girl who I shall just call "The Girl With The Worst Voice In The World." She was playing the part of Reno Sweeney because her mother had given a $5000 donation to the theater. But she couldn't sing. I mean her voice was absolutely horrible and Reno Sweeney had thirteen of the greatest songs ever written. At the end of the show I was standing next to her in a receiving line and a woman came down congratulating the cast as she approached. When she got to Terrible Singer Girl, she actually gasped and didn't know what to say. Finally she looked at the girl, smiled wildly and gave her the greatest compliment I ever heard, "Oh my, you sang so MUCH!"

Joe sold Pepsi-Cola at the Theatre. In fact he had built a whole little cabana on the patio called the Pepsi Room and even featured a picture of Joan Crawford. I told her about it and she sent him a letter which he hung next to her picture. He would do a Pepsi commercial every night during the shows' intermission and the audience looked forward to it as much as they did the show itself.

I was playing a gangster in *Anything Goes* and when Joe started his commercial, I said to the stage manager, "I think I should take my machine gun, go up and steal the Pepsi away from Joe." The stage manager said, "Don't you dare! Joe will go crazy."

I shrugged and thought "Well what could go wrong?" And so I went up with my machine gun and said, "Hand it over!" and I took the soda out of Joe's hand.

At the end of the "commercial" Joe came running off stage looking for me. He got in my face. The rest of the cast froze waiting for Joe to explode. Instead he said, "That was great! Do it every night, okay?"

I left Surflight after twelve musicals in twelve weeks with a resume, new friends and a trunkful of memories. One of the lessons Joe taught us was that if we wanted to be a success in show business, we had to put our faces in front of the people who could hire us. We should go to every audition whether we were right for the part or not because whoever was hiring might remember us for something else. Joe Hayes was an insane, bright light in my life and we stayed friends after Surflight. Joe had a deal with the Playhouse On The Mall in Paramus, New Jersey to produce children shows on Saturday afternoons. I was part of his little troupe and we would usually find out a few days before what show we were going to do. It was either *Pinocchio, Aladdin, Hansel and Gretel, Mary Poppins* or *Cinderella* because he had the costumes for them. This particular Saturday would be Aladdin and I would play the magical genii of the lamp.

We would put the outline of the show together in the van on the way to the theatre and improvised the rest.

We had a new stage manager that day and so for my first entrance a flash pot was supposed to go off letting me enter in a mysterious cloud of smoke. The flash pot ignited on cue but produced the same amount of smoke that lit match would have given when extinguished. I told the new stage manager he needed to put more powder in the charge and hopefully it would work for the second appearance.

In the next scene, Aladdin rubbed the lamp and an explosion followed that was the size of Hiroshima. I was wearing huge gold satin pants and as I stepped forward coughing, I looked down and uttered, "I am the genie of the lamp…and JESUS CHRIST MY PANTS ARE ON FIRE!"

You could see six hundred mothers covering their child's ears because the genii had just taken the name of God in vain. Sadly, Joe's contract with the Playhouse on the Mall was not renewed. But I tell you, when our little group of friends performed those children's shows, we laughed more than anybody in the audience. Joe Hayes was a man who was totally consumed by the love of show business. He never rested, never slowed down and never took care of himself. He died a few years later of a heart attack at the age of fifty-two.

I followed Joe's advice, made a daily round of the agents and casting directors so that they could get to know me and auditioned for everything. One day it paid off. I got my first big break off Broadway.

There was a new five character Israeli musical revue called *Unfair To Goliath* which was opening in about a week at the legendary Cherry Lane Theater. It was a cast of five people, written by Israel's answer to Art

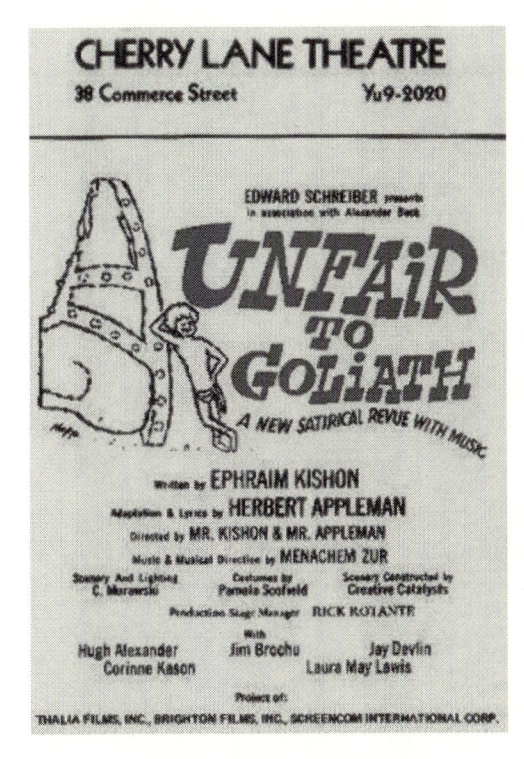

Buchwald, a fellow named Ephraim Kishon, a professorial type who was lost in the world of the commercial theatre. The sketches were based on chapters of his best-selling (in Israel anyway) book with music by Menachem Zur, who reminded me of a myopic rabbinical student.

Allen Garfield, who went on to movie fame in *Nashville* and *The Conversation*, was being fired and they needed an immediate replacement. Because I left my picture and resume at one of the producer's offices, they thought of me. I was summoned to an Upper West Side apartment where I auditioned for Kishon and Herb Appleman, the director. I sang sixteen bars of "If I Were A Rich Man" a Capella, read two scenes and within an hour I was at the Cherry Lane Theater rehearsing for my first off Broadway show.

Rehearsals came so fast because a) they had to put somebody into the show quickly and b) all of the publicity was being finalized with the posters and playbills being printed that afternoon. I had always been billed as "James" Brochu but when the poster arrived, it had been changed to "Jim." It seems to have stuck all these years.

The cast of *Unfair to Goliath*: me, Hugh Alexander, Corinne Kason, Laura Mae Lewis and Jay Devlin.

The other four members of the cast had already been rehearsing the show for three weeks so when I arrived it was like a drop of wet cement being added to a bucket that had already hardened. It seems Allen Garfield was a supreme pain in the ass. He complained about everything so the cast was very happy to see him go. They greeted me with open arms and helped in any way they could to get me up to speed.

I had an enormous amount of material to learn before the show opened in a few days. One thing I have in common with Zero Mostel is that we both lost movie parts we created on the New York stage to Topol.

In *Goliath*, I played a character named Sallah Shabati, a Polish Jew who had resettled in Israel and became a very cranky bus driver. It was truly the best sketch in the show and eventually was made into a movie called *Sallah* - with Topol playing my part. Oh Zero, I know how you feel.

But when I saw the movie of *Sallah*, I could see he was a truly brilliant actor who was done in by Norman Jewison's sluggish direction of *Fiddler on the Roof*. Many years later I met Topol after a performance of *Fiddler* in Los Angeles. I had received a nice note from him about my performance in *Zero Hour* and he invited Steve and me backstage after the show. As soon as he came out of his dressing room, I fell to one knee and I told him how great he was. He fell on one knee and told me I was greater. I prostrated myself on the floor and said, "You are greater than I." He also got prone on the floor and said, "No, you are greater." Steve turned the corner at that point and found me and Topol prone on the floor together. Wish we had a picture of that.

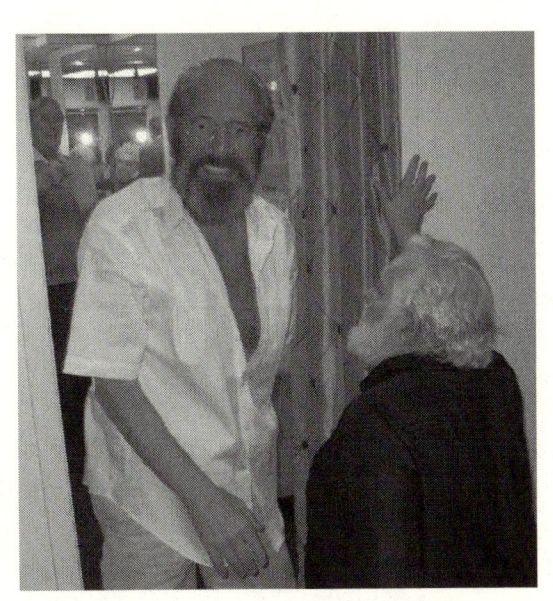

On my knees to Topol.

Unfair to Goliath got very lukewarm reviews and closed in three months. One critic said *Unfair to Goliath* is unfair to audiences. I personally got great notices which got me some attention and an agent. He sent me up for my first commercial audition and I landed it. They needed big guys who could move which qualified me to be a dancing raisin for Post Raisin Bran. It was an absolutely iconic shoot. We were all dancing in a bowl and singing "The Raisin Song." The Head Raisin was a character actor named Barney Martin who became a lifelong friend. Barney went on to great fame as "Mr. Cellophane" in the musical Chicago and as Jerry's father in the *Seinfeld* series.

Joe Hayes also ran a dinner theater in Morgan, New Jersey called *Club Bene* and he hired me for several shows there. I played Ali Hakim in *Oklahoma* opposite Carol Burnett's stepdaughter, Kathy Hamilton and *Sweet Charity* with Jeanne Lehman, who went on to have a distinguished Broadway career. A seventeen year old Larry Blank played piano for the show. He predicted that one day he would be the youngest conductor of a Broadway musical. Years later, his prediction came true when he stepped into the pit to conduct *Applause* starring Lauren Bacall.

After working with Joe Hayes for a while, he asked me if I would cast the next show he was directing at Club Bene because he couldn't be there to do it himself and he trusted me to come up with a wonderful ensemble. The show was *Bye Bye Birdie*.

We set up the audition at the Jerry LeRoy Studios on Eighth Avenue and one by one each kid came in to audition for the part of Albert, Rosie, Kim and Hugo. Toward the end of a long day, a gangly teenager came in to audition for the part of Hugo, Kim's shy boyfriend. He was tall and charismatic, unassuming, with the sweetest face and piercing blue eyes.

I forget what song he sang but he had a wonderful voice and when he read the scene I knew he had acting chops and charm to spare. I was so impressed with him that I gave him the job on the spot. He said, "Great. Now I can quit high school."

I told him if he did that, I wouldn't give him the part so he agreed and he said he would not quit. He didn't live far from the theatre and said he could do the show and go to school at the same time.

He was wonderful in the part, a real natural. I had a friend named Bob Lamond who was a manager and I wanted him to see the fellow who was playing the Dick Van Dyke part in the hope he would manage him. I drove my little VW bug out to New Jersey with David Burns in the front seat; Mary Jo Catlett and Bob Lamond in the back.

As we were going through the Lincoln Tunnel, Davy said, "What the hell show are we going to see again?" I said, "*Bye Bye Birdie*."

He roared, "Jesus Christ! Not *Bye Bye, Birdie!* I saw it with Gene Rayburn in Chicago.

It's terrible." I told him it was too late to turn back and besides it was a dinner theatre and there would be a huge buffet with a mountain of free shrimp.

On the way home I asked Bob what he thought of the fellow playing Albert? He said he made absolutely no impression but the blue eyed kid who played Hugo was "something special." I agreed. The next day Bob arranged for a meeting with the kid and took over his career. The boy's first big job was a Band-Aid commercial, then he

worked his way up to a couple of small roles on Broadway, specifically opposite The Andrews Sisters in *Over* *Here*.

Then came a movie called *Saturday Night Fever* and Johnny Travolta became one of the biggest stars on the planet. By the way he didn't listen to me and he did quit high school. I saw him a few years after that and we had a wonderful reunion. He's one of the sweetest guys you will ever meet and he was very kind about my helping in a small way to boost his career.

My friend Bob Nigro, who was one of the directors of *Search For Tomorrow*, was directing a production of *Room Service* in Kansas City and asked me if I would play Harry Binion. It was going to be a big deal. Not only was it the reopening of one of Kansas City's most beloved theatres after a multi-million dollar renovation, but it would be the first time television star Eddie Albert and his movie star son Edward would be appearing on stage together. It was also noteworthy because Edward would be playing the part his father originated on Broadway in 1937. I told Bob to count me in. I knew it would be a wonderful experience to work with two such accomplished actors. I was half right.

Eddie Albert was everything I expected him to be – charming, noble, a charismatic hail fellow well met. And Edward Albert was one of the most darling people you ever wanted to meet. We dug into rehearsals and from the first day we all knew it was not going to go well. And it didn't. Eddie was seventy-five years old and just couldn't remember the lines. Everything was so slow and nothing kills farce like slow.

The show opened on November 10, 1981 at the Folly Theater, the sister theater of the Music Box in New York - an absolute jewel. It had fallen into disarray over many years and had become a burlesque house, a porn house and was about to be torn down and made into a parking lot when a great many number of the Kansas City glitterati got together to save it.

The actress Margo, Eddie Albert's wife and star of the classic film, *Lost Horizon,* was very annoyed that the building was getting more attention than her husband and son. She confronted the society lady who had spearheaded the renovation and told her she thought she had an "Edifice Complex." When the show opened the reviews were universally terrible. Embarrassing. Bob Nigro and I went through all the notices to try and pull out a quote to use in the ads and the best we could come up with was from the Overland Park paper that declared the show was "Not a total disaster."

    I was walking to the theatre with Eddie before the Saturday matinee on November 30th when he stopped to pick up a newspaper and saw that Natalie Wood had died. He was deeply affected because RJ Wagner was his co-star on an ABC caper show called *Switch*. It was a strange matinee that afternoon. Eddie was in another world. But then, the whole experience was strange. Most of the scenes were between Eddie and me and I can still see the look in his glazed eyes trying to remember the lines.

    Many times I had to say his forgotten line which steered him back on track. We never played to more than half a house in a twelve hundred seat theater and it's tough to get a laugh when nobody else around you is laughing. It's hard to hear smiles.

Just after *Room Service* closed. I got a call from director David Guthrie who was desperately seeking an immediate replacement for an actor to play Aristide in Cole Porter's *Can-Can*. The show was being done at the Coachlight Dinner Theater in Windsor Locks, Connecticut and it seems the fellow playing the part was universally hated by the entire cast and needed to be replaced immediately. I agreed to do it.

Guthrie and his assistant ran lines with me in the car on the drive up since I had to begin performances the next night. After a quick run through, I opened without making a fool of myself and after a few shows under my belt was having a ball. It turned out it was one of those shows that lead to something greater.

One night, two fellows named Ray Golden and Al Kasha schlepped all the way from California to Connecticut to see the show. Ray was a comedy writer for the Marx Brothers and Al was a two-time Academy Award winning composer of "The Morning After" from *The Poseidon Adventure* and "We May Never Love Like This Again" from *The Towering Inferno*.

They were producing a company of *Can-Can* at the Tropicana Hotel in Atlantic City, NJ and they had come to see our version to get some ideas. The Tropicana edition was going to star the one and only Yvonne DeCarlo and would be directed by both Messrs. Golden and Kasha. But Al had never directed a show before and Ray was seventy-six years old and not well. It sent up a couple of red flags.

They told me they enjoyed my performance and would like me to join the Atlantic City team. But the downside was that my part was already cast with a fella named Russell Arms (a big star from the 1950s' *Your Hit Parade*). I would play the Head Waiter and be Russell's understudy. The money was astronomical. It was the most money I had ever been offered for a part – I mean a lot of money for nothing – so I happily agreed. It would be an open-end run by the ocean. We began rehearsals and the whole process was a mess from the start. Ray and Al together could not direct their way out of the men's room and Yvonne was a nightmare. She was functional but she was an alcoholic. She arrived drunk and she stayed drunk. It was very sad to see.

And she didn't get off to a good start with the cast either when one of the showgirls, an obvious fan, asked, "Miss DeCarlo, would you tell me about Clark Gable?"

Yvonne looked at the girl and said, "Yeah. He's dead."

Yvonne was a once-beautiful lady who had a great deal of talent but she just wasn't up to doing eight shows a week. Al, Ray and I were becoming friends and I kept suggesting line changes and directions that I thought would improve the show.

For instance, Yvonne was on stage for five minutes before anybody knew she entered. I rewrote the book to give her an entrance and then I staged it. After two days of being a backseat director, Al and Ray asked me to openly stage the show. The cast wasn't thrilled that the guy playing the head waiter was now their director and the choreographer almost mutinied. Yvonne was least happy about it.

She didn't know I had been directing the show from behind the scenes for a couple of days. The first day I actually had to do it, I told her to make a cross from one side of the stage to the other. She snapped, "Don't tell me how to act! Nobody's ever told me how to act!"

I snapped back, "Obviously!"

It was a very icy rehearsal but she followed direction and then at the day's end, came over to my table.

"I think we should have dinner tonight," she said.

I told her I thought that was a very good idea. She asked me to meet her at a restaurant called Orsini's which was on the boardwalk in Atlantic City. It was a very popular restaurant whose walls were peppered with pictures of the owner grinning with popes, presidents and all sorts of other official looking people. I got there early (as usual) but Yvonne was already there nursing a martini.

As Aristede in **Can Can**

Then we started talking and she opened up.

"I'm really nervous about this show," she told me. "I haven't been on the stage in a long time. In fact, I haven't done anything in a long time."

I reassured her she was going to be fine but, in my gut, I had real doubts.

It turned out to be a lovely evening. I came to like Yvonne very much. There wasn't anything movie star-like about her. Without the glitz and the makeup she looked like somebody's Italian mother from down the block. Like so many movie stars, she was insecure at her core. I told her I was insecure too because I had never directed a big musical before. I knew we could work together. At least that's what I had hoped.

After a few minutes, the waitress came over, looked at Yvonne and was hit by the lightning bolt of recognition.

"Oh my God! I know who you are. You're, er,…you're, er,…"

Yvonne cut her off, "Yeah. Lily Munster. Get me another drink."

Can-Can opened on September 10, 1982 and ran for almost a year. But after a few performances, Yvonne was missing more shows than she was performing and she had to be let go. At least I didn't have to be the one to do it.

Al and Ray took her aside after the second week and fired her. I think she was as relieved as we were that she was finally out of something she really didn't want to do.

She was a good lady with a good heart who had a lot of problems. Her understudy, a lady named Mary Lynn Metternich, took over the part playing opposite Russell Arms as Aristide. In a lovely twist of fate, the two of them fell in love and got married. So, something wonderful did happen out of our production of *Can-Can*.

I also met a lifelong friend doing that show, one of Broadway's greatest character actors, Robert Fitch. Bob was the original Rooster in *Annie*, has thirty-two Broadway shows under his belt and is one of the great eccentric dancers of all time.

Bob and I shared a dressing room. I came in early for a matinee (as usual) and found Bob Fosse sitting in my chair. He was in Atlantic City visiting his daughter,

Nicole, who was making her stage debut in the show as a *Can-Can* dancer.

Fosse and Fitch went way back and they were having a wonderful conversation reminiscing about all the shows they did together. A perk of show business - you never know what legend you're going to find sitting in your chair when you open your dressing room door.

Gwen Verdon, Nicole's mother, used to come down to see the show and cook spaghetti for the cast. It was terrible spaghetti but who cared? Gwen Verdon made it.

Bob Fitch (l.) drops by for a visit after a performance with Kurt Peterson, Me, Terrence McNally, Tom Kirdahy and my longtime stage manager and friend, Jeramiah Peay.

Below: "The Andrews Sisters" at Surflight with Joe Hayes as Maxine, Matt Landers at Laverne and me as Patti doing "Hold Tight."

CHAPTER EIGHT
California Here I Come

With my pals Charles Pierce and Stan Freeman at the dress rehearsal for the Hollywood Bowl tribute to Jerry Herman.

I went to California in 1975 for a two week visit and stayed on and off for almost twenty years.

My first stop was San Francisco where, through a series of unrelated incidents, I found myself in the middle of the mayoral campaign. I had a friend named Josie Lee Kuhlman who was a very wealthy lady with a home in St. Francis Woods but worked every day in the Tenderloin with the homeless. She also sat on many city commissions and was a huge advocate of women's rights.

Josie Lee decided she wanted to run for Mayor of San Francisco in 1975 and decided that I should be her campaign manager, an absolutely absurd idea as I had no experience running a political campaign. Her chances of winning were the same as mine winning an Olympic decathlon but she just wanted to get her message of social injustice across. I told her I'd be honored. She made an appointment to go see her buddy, Mayor Joe Alioto to get his endorsement.

We were ushered into his wood-paneled office and the very avuncular Mayor greeted her warmly. He looked at Josie and asked her one question, "Do you have the labor unions?"

She said she didn't.

"Forget it. You have no chance!"

He told her the race was going to be between State Senator George Moscone versus Board of Supervisors President, Dianne Feinstein. Josie had no chance of winning but if she wanted to get into the race he thought she would have a lot of fun doing it.

Every night there was a different event where George Moscone and Dianne Feinstein would give their give their spiels and take a few questions. George Moscone was a very wonderful man and everybody knew he was going to win the election.

One person who was running for Board of Supervisors showed up every night to ask for votes and hand out flyers. His name was Harvey Milk. He was a slight figure with a passionate and thoughtful nature. He couldn't participate in the mayoral debates, but he was there presenting himself on the sidewalk to anyone who would listen. He lost that year, 1975, but two years later he was elected to the Board. Sadly, we all know what happened a few years after that.

A few days after George Moscone won the election (Josie Lee got 400 votes) I decided to give Los Angeles a try. My friend Mary Jo Catlett had a spare bedroom and I could rent a little car to get me around for a few weeks.

My New York agent had relocated to L.A. and on my second day there I met him for an early breakfast at a coffee shop in Beverly Hills. He already had an audition for me to play a child molester in a movie of the week. I took the appointment information, left the restaurant on Beverly Drive, walked around the corner and stopped dead in my tracks. I couldn't believe what I was seeing. Walking toward me, in blue blazer, white shirt, ascot, hat and swinging a cane was Fred Astaire. He smiled at me and I said the stupidest thing I ever said in my life. "You're Fred Astaire!" Like he needed to know that. I told him that it was my first full day in L.A. to be an actor and mentioned that I knew Ginger from when she was in *Hello, Dolly!*

"Oh, were you in the show with her?" he asked.

"No, Mr. Astaire. I sold orange drink in the back."

He couldn't have more gracious, if confused, shook my hand and wished me luck. I watched him dance down the street believing it to be a wonderful omen. The third day in L.A. my agent called to say I had got the part. Driving on to the Paramount lot, I felt like Gloria Swanson coming back to her old studio.

All the movie magic and history was now right there in front of me. The project I booked was a three hour movie called *Law and Order* (not to be confused with the series that would come along years later) written by Dorothy Unak who was a former policewoman turned writer. Her book, about three generations of a family of New York City Irish cops, was a bestseller and now was being turned into a big all-star extravaganza for NBC.

Filming Law and Order with Darren McGavin (1976)

Darren McGavin was the star he even got to beat me up. I remember Robert Reed watching the scene and asking if I was alright as I wiped the sugarcoated blood off of my mouth.

And I couldn't believe the name of the actor on the call sheet right above mine. My brother was going to be played by an actor named James Flavin. The name probably doesn't mean anything but the face was so recognizable. He was in over five hundred and twelve movies and television shows starting with *The Airmail Mystery* in 1932, then *King Kong* in 1933. As soon as I saw him I knew I was blessed to be playing opposite this man who was a link to the Golden Age of Hollywood. He was very warm but I don't think he was well as he passed away about four or five months after we shot our scenes.

How many people can say that they got beat up by Telly Savalas? I was playing a bartender in a rough neighborhood of New York who was actually a secret police informant. Kojak was my contact and he came to the bar so I could pass the information along. But in order to keep my cover he dragged me down the length of the bars to make the hoodlums think I was under attack.

Shooting the *By Silence Betrayed* episode of *Kojak* with Sweet Telly.

Telly never rehearsed so we ran the scene with the stand-in all morning and then after lunch, Mr. Savalas appeared. He read all his lines from a cue card positioned over my shoulder. The director called, "Action," Telly entered, grabbed me by the neck and dragged me down the bar much rougher than I was expecting. When the director yelled "Cut," Telly turned into a pussycat. He put his arm around me and said, "Hey kid, I didn't hurt you did I?

"No Sir, you didn't. And it was a privilege to work with you."

"Right back at you. We'll have you on the show again, don't worry. You were good." He even gave me a lollipop.

Telly was absolutely delightful to work with, one of my fondest memories. And he was true to his word and brought me back for another *Kojak*. I played a prison warden who didn't get beat up. Besides getting work, one of the reasons I stayed un L.A. is that an old friend of mine was looking for a roommate. When I went up to look at the room he was renting, I discovered a house in the Hollywood Hills that was more than palatial - swimming pool, sundecks and all sorts of amenities. The bedroom was at the top of the house and featured a private balcony. I told him I didn't have a whole lot of money and didn't think I could afford a palace, even if it was only a room at the top of the stairs.

He asked me what I could afford. I told him about $200 a month and he said that would be fine. He would rather have the company. So all of a sudden I was living in a mansion in the Hollywood Hills and throwing marvelous parties. My thirty-first birthday was a smash. Except as I was getting my haircut for the big soiree, the announcement came over the radio that Elvis Presley was dead. Stan Freeman threw me a big party on the patio of the house and people were jumping naked into the pool. You know it's a successful Hollywood party when people jump naked in the pool.

When I told Joan Crawford I was moving to Los Angeles, she set up appointments for me to meet three of her closest friends; two to help my career and one for pure friendship.

Betty Barker

She arranged for me to meet with Vincent Sherman, the director of many classic movies including *Old Acquaintance* and *Mr. Skeffington*. He was a lovely man but really wasn't working in the movies anymore. The other "career" person Joan wanted me to meet was Herbert Kenwith who was a director for a lot of the Norman Lear shows.

The third person Joan wanted me to meet was Betty Barker who had been her secretary for over 30 years. Betty Barker had the tales of Hollywood in her as she had three bosses in her secretarial career: Eva Gabor, Joan Crawford and Howard Hughes. But she never spoke of them and she would never write that book.

Herb Kenwith became a friend and introduced me to Norman Lear's casting director, Jane Murray. She took a liking to me and gave me parts on many the Lear shows. Besides *Maude, Good Times* and *One Day At A Time*, I was a semi regular on *Mary Hartman Mary Hartman* playing officer Jerry Chandler opposite Louise Lasser.

Since I was able to hold a pencil, I've written sketches, short plays and other assorted doggerel for my own amusement but in the late 70s I thought about doing it professionally.

I showed some of my work to my pal Duane Poole who was a writer/producer for the ABC Saturday morning kids spectacular, *The Krofft Supershow,*

The show was a three hour panel that contained live action, animation and a combination of both overseen by Sid and Marty Krofft. Duane thought I would be a good fit for their live-action *Wonderbug*, a twenty minute segment about three young teens who owned a magic, broken down, flying VW Bug.

Wonderbug gave me my Writers Guild card and a credit as a Hollywood writer, even if it was for a flying VW. The luminary stage and screen writer Leonard Spigelgass welcomed the new members at our orientation. He wrote one of my favorite plays, *A Majority of One* but even more impressive, he wrote the screenplay for the film of *Gypsy*. I introduced myself and told him I was a fan of his work and that I knew we were both from Brooklyn. He invited me to his house the next day for lunch.

A small, gaunt man who looked like a rabbi without his yarmulke, he lived in one of those Hollywood classics on Benedict Canyon Drive. Lunch was more chips and pretzels but he seemed genuinely interested in my writing. Then out of the blue he said, "Are you homosexual?"

The question surprised me. "Why do you ask?"

He told me he didn't think I should be writing about gay issues. I shouldn't limit myself to that subject (though I never said I was). But I thought it was good advice not to limit myself to anything.

After a few more minutes he asked if I wanted to see the rest of the house. I should have realized what was going on when he told me we could see Danny Kaye's house from his bedroom window. Yes, the one and only time I've ever been chased around the bedroom. It must have been a sight to see a five-foot-six old, gray fox running after this six-foot four overweight gazelle.

Actually, Spigelgass was the second celebrity to chase me around a bed. But I was very fond of the other guy. He even told me he was in love with me; a very uncomfortable situation since the feeling was not mutual.

My unrequited paramour had been a major star, an enormously iconic singer whose luster had faded by the time I met him. He was now playing posh clubs and ritzy hotels around the country and Stan was conducting for him. He was still in great voice and one of the nicest guys you could ever meet.

Johnnie had a real attraction to me but there was no reciprocation. (I saw him naked in the dressing room and it wasn't pretty.)

He would try to get me up to his hotel room but it just never happened. After years of "no," he gave up and stopped talking to me. Funny, but about ten years later, Stan invited me to his house for a New Years' Eve party and I don't think he even remembered me.

But I got to sit next to Lana Turner on the piano bench that night as Stan played "Auld Lang Syne." I think you can tell I was a little bit tipsy from champagne. Oh, and my romantic pursuer was sweet Johnnie Ray, here in Philadelphia with Stan.

About a year later, the Krofft Brothers were producing a primetime variety show NBC featuring a Japanese singing duo called *Pink Lady*. *Pink Lady* was the fourth largest selling record group in the world, just

behind *ABBA*, Elvis Presley and The Beatles, but no one
in the States had ever heard of them. NBC's parent company, RCA, wanted ballyhooed so they could sell tons of records to the American public. Fred Silverman ordered six episodes of the show from the Kroffts and I was hired to be one of the six sketch writers. It was a frustrating experience because we were writing comedy sketches for two unassuming yet humorless girls who spoke no English.

Sid and Marty hired a comedian named Jeff Altman to "host" and carry the lion's share of the comedy burden. *Pink Lady*, Mei and Kei, could then just be featured doing their "bubble gum" music throughout the show. During our first production we all admitted we had never heard of *Pink Lady* and then our producer, Bonny Dore, showed us a video of stadiums filled with thousands of people going wild for them. Mei and Kei both had boyfriends back in Tokyo and had no desire to be in the States doing a TV variety show and we had to write the sketches weeks in advance so the girls could be taught their lines by rote. A lovely man named Jonathan Lucas worked with the girls every day drumming the words into their head syllable by syllable and once they learned it, we couldn't change a word.

Usually changes are made to script right up to the time the cameras roll, but we were "frozen" a week in advance. The only saving grace was all the wonderful guest stars that came to be on the show.

We had Hugh Hefner (in his silk pajamas), Larry Hagman, Lorne , Florence Henderson, Red Buttons, Robbie the Robot and Benji. One of the weekly sketch players was a fellow named Jim Varney who went on to huge movie fame with his Ernest character.

Mark Evanier, our head writer and perpetual friend, was wise to give the comedy to the guest stars. With the exception of Benji, they all spoke English.

With Marty Krofft and Pink Lady, Mei and Kei

One of our musical guests was Roy Orbison and I made a total fool out of myself working with him. I thought he was blind because he wore thick, dark glasses. I kept escorting him around the studio pushing him by the elbow when finally he turned to me and he said, "I'm not blind, you know."

Later, one of his assistants told me the history of the sunglasses. It seems when Orbison was touring with the Beatles in 1963, he left his regular glasses on a plane and had to wear sunglasses. They were cool so he made them his "look."

Our regular comedy guest star was one of my childhood heroes, Sid Caesar. For some reason, Sid asked me to work with him creating the business he would do on the show. Here I was in the same club that Mel Brooks, Neil Simon and Woody Allen all belonged to.

I would go up to his house on Alta Dr in Beverly Hills to work on sketches with him sitting at the kitchen table. When the maid came in to use the microwave, we had to get up and go to the farthest place of the house because he was terrified that the radiation from the microwave was going to kill everybody.

While we weren't working Sid would rail against that day's television comedy, especially the use of laugh tracks where "the people you hear laughing died in 1948."

We were rehearsing a sketch where Sid was playing his a piece of business with a watch. He was using a wrist-watch but I told him he could do more shtick with a pocket watch Japanese Samurai character and I gave him.

He asked for a pocket watch and was brilliant with all the different ways he used it. About ten years later I was honored to be at a luncheon where Sid and Imogene Coca were getting lifetime achievement awards. My friend Bonny Dore, the producer of *Pink Lady* and chairperson of the event, seated me at the head table with Sid and Imogene; mind blowing for a kid from the 50s.

I said to Sid, "You probably don't remember me but…"

He cut me off. "The watch. You gave me the pocket watch for the Samurai. Of course I remember you. What's your name?"

One of our other guest stars was Jerry Lewis. Before he came to the studio, all six writers came up with sketch ideas producing about a half a dozen good ones. But Jerry rejected them all before he even met us and said he knew exactly what he wanted to do. He would write his own material. First, the Kroffts should go out and rent a Chapman Crane. For those of you who don't know what a Chapman Crane is, (I didn't) a Chapman Crane is one of those huge cameras with a seated cameraman on a lift so that the camera can film high over the action and then swoop down for a closeup. So the Chapman crane was delivered followed by Jerry Lewis.

All his ideas fell flat. In fact his episode was never aired. But the thing I was most impressed with about Lewis was that at the end of the shooting day, he went around the studio and said goodbye to everybody <u>by their first name</u>.

America took *to Pink Lady* like the Spanish flu. Opposite *The Dukes of Hazzard*, the show was cancelled after two weeks. Until *The Jerry Springer Show* came along, TV Guide called *Pink Lady* the worst program in the history of television. It truly wasn't that bad. There were some moments (Red Buttons hosting a Roast of Abraham Lincoln) that transcended but not very many.

Both girls were absolutely delightful but just wanted to go home and let people in stadiums scream at them.

For some reason, I was growing a beard during the *Pink Lady* job which came in handy when I got a call from Bob Nigro asking me if I wanted to go to Kansas City to play Tevye in the Waldo Astoria production of *Fiddler on the Roof*.

Playing Tevye was one of the great joys of my life.

I was off in a flash and had one of the greatest experiences of my life. The Waldo Astoria dinner theater was run by two entrepreneurs named Dennis Hennessy and Richard Carruthers. They were both passionate about theater, savvy about theatre and produced exceptional star-driven shows on a postage stamp sized stage.

Playing Tevye made me realize my heart was in New York. Also, my dad was starting to decline and I thought I should be closer to him. Then came a life-changing incident; the *Fiddler* experience accidentally turned me into a playwright.

One day I was talking to producer Richard Carruthers who was telling me about the next play they were producing. I told him I thought it was a terrible play. He said, "It took the writer two years to write that play."

I bet him I could write a bad play in a week and so I rented a typewriter and wrote a play I called *Cookin' With Gus*. I sent it to Samuel French and Company and they published the damn thing. So that was the beginning of my life as a playwright. *Cooking with Gus* is a terrible play. Absolutely terrible. I have no qualms about saying that. It's an absolute dinner theater formula: four characters, three acts, two intermissions, one set and no plot.

The story is about a lady named Gus Richardson who's afraid to speak on a microphone. It was loosely based on two *I Love Lucy* plots sewn together. Gussie is one of the world's greatest chef's who's offered a TV Cooking show. But she has crippling stage fright and can't do it. Her husband hypnotizes her out of the problem. Pure dinner theater faire, but the damn thing has now been done in several countries and was filmed for French HBO as *Les Pieds Dans Les Plats*. Recently, it became part of the repertory of the State Theatre in Turkey. I hear I'm very big in Istanbul.

While I was in California I made friends with three men all named Charles: all funny, all famous and all very complicated. They were Charles Nelson Reilly, Charles Pierce and Rip Taylor, whose real name was Charles Elmer Taylor. Pierce and Reilly were both alcoholics. They held up a mirror to my own drinking problem which reared its ugly head from time to time.

I met Charles Nelson Reilley in 1964 when he was doing *Dolly*! and his dressing room was next to Davy Burns

. But we reconnected when he was directing Stan Freeman's one man show about Oscar Levant, *At Wit's End*. Reilly was a charming host, inviting us to his boat or to dinner parties at his house. Charles was a very funny, very acerbic and a very loving friend until he had one gin too many and then he could become a screaming, horrible monster.

Most people know Charles as the silly game show personality but he was actually a very brilliant acting coach and director. He had many Broadway credits including Julie Harris's *The Belle of Amherst*.

I went to a few of his acting classes and could see why everybody raved about him. There was a girl in the class who was very needy and got on everyone's nerves, especially Charles. On one occasion she was going to be playing Juliet in a production of *Romeo and Juliet* and was stressing about the part. She stopped the class cold and said, "Excuse me Mr. Reilly but do you think Romeo and Juliet had carnal relations?"

He stopped for a moment and said, "Well, in the Chicago company they did!"

Charles invited us to the opening of our friend Stan Freeman's play, *At Wits' End* at the Coronet Theatre on La Cienega. I brought Lucille Ball and Charles arranged for Steve to escort Abagail Van Buren, better known as "Dear Abby."

In the show, Stan played Oscar Levant and besides being able to show off his unparalleled piano skills, he was able to chew on his comic chops as well. It was a masterful performance.

Charles arranged a small dinner for us after the show at Orso's in Beverly Hills and we drove over with Lucy in the front seat with Steve and Abby in the back. On the way over, Abby said you know I liked the show but I just had a few ideas that might make the show better. do you think he'd be interested in hearing them?" I knew he wouldn't. The last thing a performer wants is notes. But I said, "Oh yes. You must."

We sat down at the restaurant and after a while there was a lull in the conversation and I nodded to Abby indicating this would be a good time to speak up. Dear Abby said, "Stan I liked the show a lot but I had some ideas that might make it better." The moment I had hoped for arrived. I turned to Dear Abby and said, "Who the hell are you to give advice?"

We were all having a wonderful time at Sardi's one night when suddenly he turned and said he hated all of us and we could pay our own bills and he left. And then he didn't remember what he had done.

I produced his one man show, *Save It For The Stage: The Life Of Reilly*, at the El Portal Theater in Los Angeles. He was impossible to work with. The show was running over three hours and fifteen minutes and his New York producer and director were begging for cuts.

We sat in his dressing room one night after the show. He never drank before performance but as soon as the curtain came down, out came the flask with the bourbon. So the two of them sat in the dressing room begging him to cut at least 1/2 hour out of the show before they took it to New York. He kept saying,

"But I can't cut anything. It's all too good."

His director, Paul Linke, was brutal. "It's not all too good. You gotta cut twenty minutes!"

At that point Charles said calmly, "Jimmy would you drive me home? Thank you." We left without saying goodnight. The atmosphere was totally silent as we got into the car and drove up Coldwater Canyon Drive. He had not said a word during the whole trip but just kept sipping his bourbon. When we got to the top of Mulholland Drive he screamed, "They're the Ramseys and I'm Jon Benet and they're killing me!" We're lucky I didn't drive off the cliff.

Steve and I were shopping at the Gelson's supermarket on Laurel Canyon one afternoon when I spotted Charles Pierce in Aisle 8: Fruits and Vegetables. He was one of the most famous female impressionists in my lifetime and I was a huge fan of his. He stood there comparing bunches of grapes – either to eat or wear on his head when he impersonated Carmen Miranda. Of course almost nobody would know him out of his drag but I approached him and introduced myself.

We had a lot of mutual friends and spent almost an hour talking among the avocados. Steve and I invited him to a party we were having the following Saturday. He came, we bonded and the rest is history. Charles Pierce and I developed a very close friendship. We spoke every day at 10:00 AM which we called "The Morning Report," Charles was happiest when he could start the day by saying, "Well guess who hit the linoleum today?"

One of our favorite outings was to go up to Forest Lawn and visit the tomb of Betty Davis. It may sound macabre but the Forest Lawn Cemetery is one of the most beautiful spots in Los Angeles, high on a Hill overlooking Warner Brothers.

Charles Pierce: "Guess who hit the linoleum today?"

One night, Steve and I were having dinner with Charles at the place called the Venture Inn on Ventura Blvd in Studio City. The restaurant had three large banquettes with three wall-sized pictures over each one: Marilyn Monroe, Joan Crawford and Charles Pierce as Bette Davis. We sat in the booth under Charles' photo.

After a few minutes. a group came in and sat opposite us and was talking about the photos. One pointed to the picture over our table and didn't realize that Charles was sitting there under his own face. Charles called over to the table and said, "Excuse me, do you know who that is in the picture?"

Charles was very pleased when the guy said, "Yes! That's the great Charles Pierce. Charles was less thrilled when the guy added, "He's dead!"

Sometimes Charles would bring Bea Arthur along when we'd go out for dinner and she enjoyed our company – especially Steve. One day, Steve had just gotten out of the hospital and was lying on the couch asleep when Bea and Charles came over to see how he was doing. Steve slept through most of the visit but as he regained consciousness he looked up and saw Bea sitting in my chair and said, "Oh God, I was dreaming and thought I was Betty White."

Bea had a favorite joke about Cinderella who is invited to the ball but her fairy godmother says, "If you're not home by midnight, I'm going to turn your pussy into a pumpkin."

Cinderella got to the ball and met the most handsome man then a few minutes before the witching hour struck she said to him, "I have to go."

The handsome young man grabbed her and said, "But I love you and I don't even know your name."

She said, "I'm Cinderella. Who are you?"

He said, "I'm Peter Peter Pumpkin Eater."

Bea would take a long pause at this point and (as Cinderella) say, "Well, maybe just a few more minutes."

I have no idea How I Met Charles "Rip" Taylor. It seems like I just knew him forever. When he was a kid, he had been horrifically abused by his prostitute mother. One night Steve was in tears listening to Rip tell about all the things that his mother had done to him and allowed others if they gave her an extra couple of bucks.

I really liked Rip. I considered him a good friend but he had the kind of energy that drained the life out of you if you were around it too long. He needed a lot of attention.

When Rip was putting his one man show together he asked me to meet him for breakfast at the Sportsmen's in Studio City. He handed me the script of his one man show, called *It Ain't All Confetti,* and said, "I want you to direct it." I said, "Rip, I mean this from the bottom of my heart; I would rather have hot needles poked in my eyes."

I suggested another friend of mine and Rip hired him to direct. That person hasn't spoken to me since. Rip would call him twenty times a day with ideas or line changes.

But he was always there when I needed him for a benefit, throwing confetti and generating comic bedlam. I was producing a tribute to Donald O'Connor at the El Portal Theatre and asked Rip to appear with Carol Channing, Edie Adams, Kathleen Freeman and myself. Just before we all went on, Carol started singing, "Why-O-Why-O-Why-O? Why did I ever leave Ohio?" from *Wonderful Town*, a show she did with Edie in 1957.

One night Steve and I were at home when the phone rang. It was Charles Nelson Reilly. He wanted to talk about his show. Just as he started talking, we were interrupted by the call waiting beep. I put Charles on hold and found Rip on the other line. I said to Steve, "I got the two biggest Queens in Hollywood on the same line at the same time!" Steve took a wonderful Bea Arthur pause and said, "Three!"

In 1982, I was writing for a now defunct humor magazine called *Comedy*. They asked me to do an interview column and I suggested that I interview one of the Kings of Hollywood comedy Hal Roach because a) I had always wanted to meet him and b) at age 90, I wasn't sure how much time he had left.

A friend had his phone number and so I called the house and his nurse answered. His wife Lucile had died the year before. The nurse said she thought Hal would love to talk about his career but because of health issues, he could only give me 15 or 20 minutes. I thought that amount of time was better than nothing and quickly accepted. A few days later I drove to his house on Bellagio Road in Bel Air and was greeted by a pleasant yet stern nurse who underscored that I could only have the agreed upon half-hour. I already got a ten minute extension.

Mr. Roach was sitting in an overstuffed chair in his very unassuming living room and shook my hand with a grip that belied his ninety years. The nurse asked me if I would be comfortable enough to let myself out after the half-hour as she had some errands to do and it was the housekeeper's day off. I assured her I could and she left Mr. Roach and myself alone. We bantered a bit with him asking me questions about my career and as soon as the nurse made her exit and the door clicked shut, Mr Roach looked at me and said, "Got a cigarette?"

I did. He said, "They don't let me smoke when hatchet-face is around. They're not menthol, are they?"

"No, sir. Pall Mall king size."

"Good," he smiled. "Pull off that damn filter will you?"

I pulled off the damn filter and lit up our smokes. When the nurse came back three hours later, we were still talking. She pretended not to notice that the room was filled with dense cigarette smoke because between the two of us, we had almost finished off a pack. But there I was with the man who put Laurel and Hardy together, created Our Gang and produced some of the most enduring dramas of the Golden Age of Hollywood. Here are some of the highlights of that talk.

I asked him how he felt when he read about himself as was of the founding pillars of Hollywood? He said, I would much rather be making something funny than read about what I did 40 years ago. My forte is visual comedy. It's the things that people do that are funny and not what they say. In all the pictures I ever made the dialogue was written by somebody else, not me. There were great visual comedians and great oral ones. For example, Bob Hope is tops at oral comedy but his visual comedy is very mediocre.

I told him I once read that Harold Lloyd didn't think he was funny and that it was Roach who told him he was.

"That's right," he said. "Harold Lloyd wasn't funny. He was a hell of an actor and worked like hell. He always played the young boy. Even when he was older. I had to let him go because he wouldn't, couldn't let me age his character. He was so wrapped up in the young guy he played. He and I were extras together making pictures at Universal when I first met him and he was devoted to improving himself. That's what impressed me. As far as I'm concerned the greatest thing that Harold Lloyd ever did for me was, for instance, he would turn to me and say, 'What do I _do_ that's funny here?' And if I didn't have something we all waited until I came up with it. He didn't create bits on his own. If I said the bits were funny he accepted that. It's ironic that for all the laughter he engendered, Harold Lloyd didn't have a great sense of humor. He also only had two fingers on his right hand which made his athletic feats so extraordinary."

I told him that I went to see a Lloyd film before our talk and didn't notice his hand. Roach said, "He had a prosthetic glove that made his hand look whole, but when he was hanging off buildings (as he did) it was with two fingers.

I asked him, "What's humor, Mr. Roach? What makes people laugh?" He answered quickly, "It's juxtaposition. I think the greatest example of it was in a Laurel and Hardy film. A family loses a painting of "The Blue Boy." Stan and Ollie find a horse named Blue Boy. When they ask the family where to put it the wife says, "Put it on the piano!" Hardy leads the horse into the house and knocks over a statue of a woman that breaks into three parts. Hardy rearranges the three broken pieces so that is her head is on the bottom, the feet are in the middle and the torso is on the top. Laurel sees it and accepts it because he believes that rich people know so much more."

"Why is getting hit in the face with a pie funny?"

"It's not," he said. "What's funny is <u>who</u> throws the pie and <u>who</u> gets hit with it. You have to like the guy who throws it and hate the guy who gets it. if you don't know who threw it or who gets it, it's not funny. If you write from a comedy angle you must show the who and the why."

I told him I once read an article where he said actors become the characters they play. What did he mean? "I saw Jimmy Stewart on a talk show the other night. I don't know if he knows it or not but he's playing a character that he developed - the way he talks and all. Originally he wasn't that way. Gary Cooper started with me as an extra and he wasn't that way. He developed a mannerism so they became Gary Cooper. It became his character off the screen and on the screen as well." His nurse, "Old Hatchet Face" gave me the heave-ho after our half hour together became three. But I could have actually waited ten years to do that interview…Hal Roach lived to be 100.

Stan Harris was a marvelous television director who asked me to be his assistant on a new project that he was involved with. I really didn't know how or want to be an assistant director until he told me about the show. Stan really didn't need and assistant but thought I would enjoy just being there. And he was so right.

The PBS show was called *Musical Comedy Tonight* and it was being produced and hosted by Sylvia Fine, the wife of Danny Kaye. I only had one memorable encounter with Danny Kaye which was at Cedar Sinai Hospital in Los Angeles. Barry Vigon and I went to visit Mary Jo Catlett who recovering from knee replacement surgery. We left her room, got in the elevator and the door opened on the next floor. In walked Danny Kaye. Barry was so thrilled he gushed, "Oh Mr. Kaye, I have to tell you that *The Court Jester* is my most favorite movie in the world." Without batting an eye Danny Kaye glared at him and said, "Really? Then you ought to have your fucking head examined." The ride to the ground floor was excessively cool.

The premise of *Musical Comedy Tonight* was, as Sylvia Fine explained, was the recreation of "Four hits, four runs, four eras." A half hour was dedicated to each of the four shows Sylvia picked: Good News featuring Sandy Duncan and Bobby Van representing the 1920s, *Anything Goes* featuring Ethel Merman for the 1930s, *Oklahoma* with John Davidson and Carol Burnett (1940s) and the 1970s *Company* with Richard Chamberlain and Bernadette Peters.

Stan Harris said there would be one more special guest who Sylvia would interview – Agnes DeMille. Who could say no to working with that lineup?

Merman arrived for the taping at the Wilshire Ebell Theatre and I met her at the stage door with my mandatory clipboard in hand. She looked at me and said, "Little Jimmy Brochu? Mother of God, what are you doing here?" First, I had to laugh when she called me "little," then I told her I was the director's assistant and anything she needed I'd be happy to get. She said, "Well, we'll go out for a drink after."

I brought a picture of her that some friends had given me for my birthday so she could autograph it for me. It was a publicity still from the 40s with Ethel standing in front of an NBC microphone, her hand clutched belting out a number.

We taped the *Good News* section which went off without a hitch. Sylvia interviewed Agnes de Mille who told about creating the ballets for *Oklahoma* and how the hand gestures were fluttering hearts soaring to the Sky. Then we began taping the *Anything Goes* section. She sang a flawless "I Get A Kick Out Of You" and a duet with Rock Hudson on "You're The Top."

Then it was time to tape the big title number with a chorus of twenty singers and dancers. Ethel came to the front of the stage, Peter Matz raised his baton, the music orchestra played the introduction and she stood there looking confused. Merman said, "What song is this?" Peter Matz thought she was kidding and said, "Anything Goes, Ethel."

Merman looked down at him and said, "I don't know that song. Why are you giving me songs I don't know!" Everybody froze. How could Ethel Merman not know "Anything Goes?" Stan ran down the aisle, jumped on the stage and took her aside. Then he turned to me a whispered in my ear, "Take her to her dressing room tell her we have a technical problem." I did as Stan asked, told her to rest and I would be back. Twenty minutes later I knocked and heard that Clarion voice, "Come in."

She asked if the problem had been solved and I said it had. I walked her back to the stage, Peter Matz struck up the orchestra and Ethel tore into "Anything Goes" with the same power she had when she introduced the song.

After the number I brought her back to the dressing room and asked her to autograph the picture I brought. She was surprised when she saw it and said, "Where the hell did you get this?" I told her a friend gave it to me for my birthday. She said, "Jimmy, that's no friend." She started to sign it and I could see her hand was shaking. I think she had a mini-stroke that day and she would die of a brain tumor a few years later.

She told me she was too tired to go out for a drink and hoped I understood. Before we left, I gave her a goodbye kiss and said, "Ethel, do you remember the day your dad brought me backstage after *Gypsy* to meet you for the first time?

She looked at me with sad eyes and said, "Honey, I don't remember yesterday." It was the last time I saw her.

The previous picture was taken in Dinah Shore's dressing room on August 16, 1976, my thirtieth birthday. She was taping a show at Television City and I went over to visit her. She invited me and a few others out to a Chinese restaurant for dinner and after we all sat down she looked at us and said, "I don't share." Ethel's chow mein was hers and hers alone. I worked with Jack Klugman who told me a great Merman story. He said, "I'm not a singer so when we were doing *Gypsy* and I had to sing a song with her, I kept holding back. She kept saying, 'Come on, Jack. Sing out!' Finally we got to the first preview in Philadelphia and I decided I was going to sing at the top of my lungs. When we got off stage Ethel pushed me against the wall and said, 'What the hell are you doing, Jack. This is <u>my</u> duet'"

CHAPTER NINE
Farewell Dad, Hello Steve

Steve and I on the day we met on the Galileo May 26, 1985.

Doing *Can-Can* in Atlantic City gave me a chance to visit my father more often. He had gotten feeble and never cleaned the house. He said after you let the dust go for three months it didn't matter.

Dad was a heavy smoker all of his life, two or three packs a day since he was fourteen. Whenever I came for a visit, I would open the door and be hit in the face by a wall of acrid smoke.

I knew something was wrong during one visit when he couldn't stop coughing. I took him to a doctor a friend recommended, (he didn't have his own) who diagnosed him with lung cancer and gave him about three months to live. I decided to move back to his place so I could take care of him and be my parent's parent.

I was truly scared for the first time in my life because even though I was making a living and being an adult on my own he still took care of me. Every once in a while he would help out with a couple of extra bucks just to make sure I had money in my pocket.

But this was about to stop and I didn't know what my future was going to be like. I was really looking for somebody else or something to take care of me. I settled upon my old faithful childhood friend, Mother Church. A job in the church was security. I need a place to hide out. Then I could figure out what I was hiding from. But the priesthood offered a hiding place <u>and</u> security.

I thought if I was going to be a priest I should at least go to church. I hadn't been in many years so I started to attend services at Blessed Sacrament Church on West 71st St. After a few visits, the pastor, Fr. Ed McCarrey, noticed me. He was a gaunt, abstemious man with a sallow skin who looked like he was setting the alter for his own funeral.

I told him I was thinking about becoming a priest. He looked at me like raw meat. But I confided that I worried I wouldn't be accepted because I was in my mid-thirties. He disagreed. He said I had several good years left and the Church needed guys like me. I didn't want to tell him that I was only doing it for lifelong room and board and dressing up for high mass on Sunday.

Father Ed invited me to come to the rectory to talk to him and after about five minutes I realized he was as big a show queen as I was. We weren't talking about Scripture and the Fathers of the Church; we were arguing whether *Hello, Dolly!* or *Funny Girl* had a better book.

He arranged a meeting with the vocation director, a pudgy, smiley priest in his mid-thirties who obviously had too much sacramental wine at morning mass.

After a series of psychological tests and interviews, I was accepted into the bosom of Mother Church with such speed it made the new Roman collar spin around my neck. It also gave me a chance to be closer to dad who was now in Calvary Hospital in the Bronx.

Lung cancer is a horrible disease that generously provides a torturous death. I wept for my dad as he struggled to breathe. I used to love to buy cigarettes out of a vending machine for him when I was a kid. *Red Pall Mall* was his brand. That's the one with no filters. I was in the seminary when my father died and the church gave him quite a sendoff. All the priests and seminarians gathered at the church. My father had no close friends at the end so it was heartwarming to see the church filled. As I followed my father's casket out of the church, I looked at my fellow seminarians and thought, "Okay, now how do I get out of this!"

While I was in the seminary Terence Cardinal Cooke died and was replaced by Cardinal John J. O'Connor, whose philosophy was just to the right of Attila the Hun. We were all invited to be a part of his installation service at Saint Patrick's cathedral. I was standing with one of my fellow seminarians when he spotted Mother Teresa coming out of the Cathedral. He said, "I have to get her autograph."

I said, "What are you crazy? Mother Teresa doesn't give out autographs. That's Mother Teresa, not Cher. Despite what I said he ran over to her, thrust the program in her face and said, "Hello, Mother Teresa. Could I please have your autograph?" Without missing a beat, she took the program, reached under the fold of her habit, pulled out a sharpie and with huge flourish signed *La Teresa* and walked away. I guess it wasn't the first time she ever gave an autograph.

One thing I enjoyed about the seminary was that it was like a big gay boarding house with secret sex visits occurring on a regular basis. I actually fell in love with a straight seminarian almost twenty-years my junior.

He was a beautiful guy in every way. Even though he was Straight, we developed a sexual relationship that was one of the most passionate I've ever known.

My Seminary class, The blond fellow on my right stayed with it. He's John Barres, now Bishop of Rockville Center, Long Island.

He surprised me at my father's wake the night before the funeral. He told me he thought I would need him. We went back to my father's apartment and made love until a few hours before the service. (Sidebar: He also left the church, married a beautiful girl and had scads of kids. I follow him secretly on social media and think of him often with great fondness.

There were only a few more weeks left in the semester and after my father died I realized I had made a big mistake. It was a cowardly thing to do. How could I be a priest if I wasn't a Catholic. When we said the words of the Creed, I believed in absolutely nothing I was saying. The seminary had only reinforced my belief as an atheist and as George Carlin says, "All religion is a form of mental illness." So after the first semester, I left.

I cleaned out dad's apartment, said goodbye to Bay Ridge, went back to my little studio apartment on 69th St. and wondered if I could get my career back. My old agents were happy to have me and I started writing a new play and called it *The Lucky O'Learys*. I couldn't realize how important that play would become in my life.

A few months after I left the seminary I needed to get away for a few days. I had forgotten I had signed up for a Discount Travel Club and called their hotline to see if there was any enticing deals. Maybe a cruise?

The offer that attracted me most was a five day Memorial Day Weekend Cruise from New York to Bermuda on the *SS Galileo*. The astonishing price of this adventure was only $200; $40 bucks a day. It was so cheap I called my friend Jimmy Rilley and asked him to go with me.

I always loved being on the ocean. There's something mystical about standing on the bow of a ship on a moonless night, embraced by the awesome blackness that makes you feel like a speck in the vast universe. Then you go inside and Cha-Cha.

The *Galileo* was built for the old Italian line as the *Galileo Galilei*. It was a gorgeous ship with sleek lines and mid-century motifs. But it had obviously seen better days and I knew immediately that I wasn't in the Queens Grill on the QE2..

But still, it was always relaxing to be on the ocean and I had never been to Bermuda before. The first night out I went to the Fantasy Lounge; the romantic meeting place for the honeymooning couples and young lovers and it was lit like a night game at Yankee Stadium. The light was blinding.

There was a young couple doing their act in the middle of the dance floor, a sort of old Music Hall routine that combined tap dancing, singing and xylophone. They were young, blonde and looked like a brother and sister act. I found out later they were The Musical Derricks, a young newlywed couple from England.

When they finished, a very handsome young man sat down at the piano and began his set. He looked a little snotty but he was a good singer so I ordered a Dewar's on the rocks and sat in the back of the room to listen. He opened his set with "One More Kiss" from *Follies*.

I nursed my Scotch and sang along. At his break he came over and said, "I saw you singing 'One More Kiss.' How do you know that song?" I told him I worked in the theatre and Follies was one of my favorite shows. We talked. We talked some more. After five days I had fallen in love with him. He not so much with me but I think he saw the potential in the relationship. We had an almost hilarious attempt at sex on the last night but it was never about that. I told him if he thought we should be together to meet me at Lifeboat 8 at 8:00 o'clock the next morning. He said he would think about it, we kissed and went our separate ways.

At 8:00 o'clock the next morning I was on the Lifeboat Deck standing in front of Lifeboat 8 and when 8:30 came I felt like Cary Grant in *An Affair to Remember* waiting at the top of the Empire State building for Deborah Kerr. No Steve. As I started to leave, I ran into my friend Jimmy Rilley and he said, "Oh there you are. Steve has been looking all over the boat for you."

When I finally found Steve on the other side of the ship he said he had forgotten which lifeboat he was supposed to meet me at. Yay! He wasn't rejecting me. He was a Space Cadet. It was a trait I would learn to love over the years. Sometimes, he would go on concert tours and I would have to pin his destination to his coat so he could remember where he was going.

After Steve said, "yes," he had five more weeks to go on his Galileo contract. He could get a special rate ($30 a day for a really nice cabin) and so I took many cruises on the ship in the five weeks he had remaining.

The Xylophone couple, Adam and Nicky Derrick, whose real names were Adam and Nicky Wright, were his best friends and they became two of mine as well. Eventually they became important players in the cruise industry and gave me my first opportunity to be a cruise ship lecturer which opened the whole world to us.

At the end of his contract, Steve moved into the little apartment on 69th St which was probably five hundred square feet, room enough for the two of us and my cat, Howard Katz. We spent a whole year in that apartment before we decided to move to California, driving across the country with Howard perched in the rear window of the cat like a bobble head toy.

We always joked that we got together because I was looking for a free accompanist and he was looking for a free apartment. Whatever works.

A few weeks after Steve moved in, my friend Jacqueline Babbin became the producer of *All My Children.* Jackie won the Emmy for the TV movie of *Sybil* starring Sally Field and now was going to take the helm of the ABC soap opera. She hired me to play kindly Father James, a private joke since she always thought it was ridiculous I had ankled off to be a priest.

One of my scene partners became a member of our little family of friends, Ruth Warrick. Ruth's big claim to fame was playing Emily Norton Kane in *Citizen Kane* opposite Orson Welles in the 1941 classic. And she had been playing Phoebe Tyler Wallingford on *All My Children* for over 30 years. A very funny incident involved both Charles Pierce and La Warrick. Ruth was going to be honored for her 75th birthday at the Bonaventure Hotel in Los Angeles. It was going to be a star studded affair and Ruth invited Steve, myself and Charles Pierce to be with her at the event.

At Ruth Warrick's 75th Birthday Party at the Bonaventure Hotel in Los Angeles with Charles Pierce, Ruth, me, producer James A. Doolittle and Ann Miller.

    Ruth looked absolutely stunning that night. She had a whole team of makeup and hair people working on her for hours and the result was glorious, a real movie star. Even Ann Miller couldn't outshine her that night.
    One of the features of the evening was a live auction for some very seriously-priced paintings. Charles could not be at the same table with us and was about two tables away.

He kept standing up and waving over to us throughout the night but after a couple of drinks, he didn't realize the fine arts auction had begun. As one of the paintings was about to be sold, Charles jumped up and waved at us again. Over the loudspeaker we heard the auctioneer say, "And sold to Charles Pierce for $40,000!" Charles screamed "No! No! I was just schmoozing!" and sat down rather quickly. The whole thing was straightened out later but we were all on the floor laughing. That is all of us but Charles

The second move to California was the right one. Steve got a job almost immediately as the Managing Director of the National Academy of Songwriters, a nonprofit organization that helped aspiring songwriters' network with more successful ones. It was a chance to work with many of the most notable names in the industry.

Every year Steve would produce a show called *The Salute To The American Songwriter* which would honor a famous songwriter or songwriting team. He had the good sense to hire me to write and direct the shows which gave me an opportunity to work with folks like Peter Allen, Stevie Wonder and James Brown among others. They were all absolute delights and I got a kick out of the "Hardest Working Man in Show Business" who kept saying to me, "You're my man!"

There was a lovely, attractive gal named Blythe Newlon who worked with Steve at NAS who was in charge of developing new artists. One day a dashing aspiring singer-songwriter came in to join the organization and gave Blythe a CD of his music. Blythe fell in love with his music as well as its composer who turned out to be a very shy but fascinating guy. Steve saw that they both liked each other and decided to play matchmaker, nudging them to take their relationship a step further.

The four of us, Steve and I and Blythe and her boyfriend Danny, went out for dinner one night and I asked him how his career was going. He said he thought that he didn't see a future for himself in the music industry so he decided to move back East and teach at a Prep School in New Hampshire. He told me he thought he'd be good at writing a thriller and what should he do? I told him the only way to learn how to write is to write. So he married Blythe, moved back to New Hampshire and wrote his thriller. It did okay. His second book did a little better. His third book was a best seller and his fourth book became a world-wide phenomenon. Perhaps you've heard of *The DaVinci Code*? Yes, Blythe's boyfriend, then husband was Dan Brown.

One of the worst experiences of my life was working for Disney. They bought a pilot from me called *Louie* which I had written for comedian Louie Anderson.

But in Disney's infinite wisdom they thought it would be much better if it was about a thirteen year old boy. With each meeting I approached the Disney lot with a Pluto-sized knot in my stomach just wanting it to all be over.

The young man who was assigned to help me "develop" the project was about eighteen years old, a nerdy Jewish kid with terrible ideas who years later became the head of one of the major television networks. He was a paradigm of how to dumb things down. Steve and I celebrated when CBS passed on *Louie* and Mickey Mouse and I were free of each other.

The characters in *The Lucky O'Learys* were based upon two aunts of mine who had a sibling rivalry since they were little girls. The play was published by Sam

French and Steve put together some high-profile readings to see if we had anything worthwhile. I was blessed to have some of the best actors on the planet do it: Pat Carroll, Kathleen Freeman, Doris Roberts, William Schallert, Helen Hunt, Allyn Ann McLerie, George Gaynes, Charles Esten, Dermot Mulroney and Kevin McCarthy. The play got wonderful reactions and I thought I'd have a better chance to get it produced if I attached a star to it. So I sent *The Lucky O'Learys* to Kate Hepburn and about a week later received a note. She always typed them herself. And I love the way she referred to the play as "The Irish Piece." She did exactly what she said and she sent the script to a producer friend of hers, a mensch of a man named Merrill Karpf, who had produced, among other things, *Stone Pillow* starring Lucille Ball. Working with Lucille Ball would be a fantasy come true. She was the one who taught me everything I knew about comedy. The idea was so out of reach, I couldn't allow myself to think about it. But then I thought, what the hell?

Steve and I got her address from a Maps To The Stars Homes and there it was: 1000 North Roxbury Drive in Beverly Hills. I wrote a note to Lucy, telling her I was a student at her six-week Sherwood Oaks Comedy Seminar in 1977 and (this was the clincher), I played Backgammon.

I attached the note to a manuscript of the play, drove over to her house and put it in her mailbox. A few days later the telephone rang and it was Lucy herself. She read the play and told me it was the first time she laughed out loud in months. Could I come over to the house and talk about it? Later I found out that Merrill had already talked to her about me so I had been "vetted."

I went over to her house the next day. She greeted me at the front door in white slacks and blouse, that shock of red hair and those red bow lips. Her baby blues were obstructed by dinner-plate sized sunglasses.

The Salute to the American Songwriter Show gave me the opportunity to work with Peter Allen, Stevie Wonder and James Brown

We walked past the pool to the back house to play backgammon and talk about the script. I sat down opposite her and bang, I broke her chair. I said, "Excuse me, Miss Ball, but...."

She stopped me, "Lucy! Call me Lucy."

"Okay Lucy," I continued, "I broke your chair."

She seemed surprised but then said, "Well, take another one. So I took another chair, sat down and broke that one too. This time she heard the crack and I could see her thinking, "What the hell did I get myself into?"

I pointed to a third chair and said I would take that one because it looked sturdy. She said, "The other two looked sturdy too."

I fetched the third chair, sat down and we both held our breath. It held. After five hours of playing backgammon, I won the match by a dollar. She said, "But we haven't talked about your play. I love your play and hope we can do it. Can you come back tomorrow?"

My heart exploded but I tried to remain calm. I said, "Yes, but tomorrow is my birthday so if I come back you have to give me a present."

She took a pause and said, "Maybe I'll give you a chair."

I came back the next day and when we had a pause in our game, she went to the corner of the room and came back with a small cupcake complete with lit candle singing *Happy Birthday*. I really started to get teary. She said, "Why are you crying?" I said, "Well did Lucille Ball ever sing Happy Birthday to you?"

Then she gave me a green foil-wrapped box which contained a souvenir watch with a caricature of her face on it. There was a card that read, *Jim - I will always have time for you - Love Lucy.*

From then on I spent just about every day with Lucy who became one of my most cherished friends. I've written a whole book about Lucy so I'm not going to write a lot about her here. But I do want to add a few thoughts I couldn't express thirty years ago.

I didn't write much about her second husband, Gary Morton so let me describe him in a few words: controlling, greedy, sneaky, overbearing, jealous, lowlife. I did an interview about the book with the great radio personality George Putnam who many say was the inspiration for the character of Ted Baxter on *The Mary Tyler Moore Show*. Before we went on air George said, "What's your opinion of Gary Morton." I expressed how I felt and he said, "Good judge of character. I met him once and took a permanent pass."

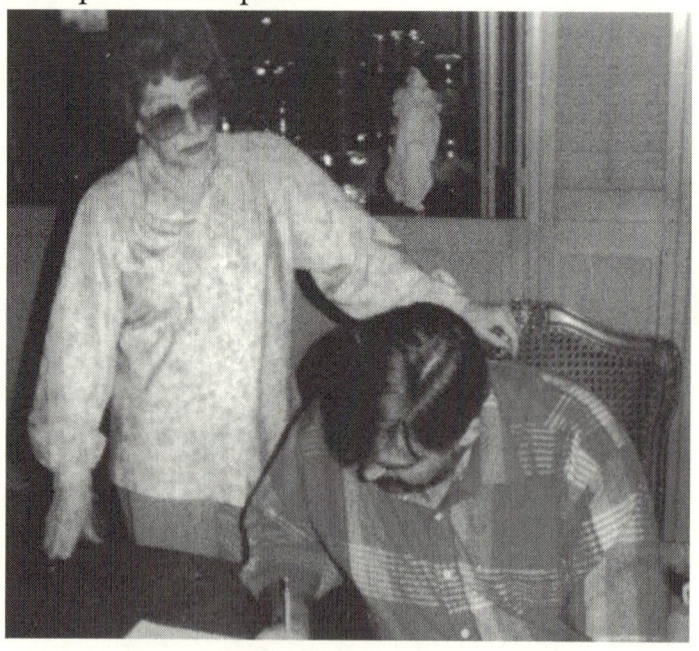

Lucy checking my math as I add up our backgammon score.

Lucy was looking for a project to do with Audrey Meadows and she thought *The Lucky O'Learys* would be a perfect fit. She had Gary call the head of 20th Century Fox and we drove over to meet, Gary and me, in his ostentatious silver Bentley. Lucy drove a gold Mercedes that matched her hair. Gary was very impressed with himself and needed a car that fit the size of his ego which could be seen only from the air.

> **Katharine Houghton Hepburn**
>
> I - 5 - 1988
>
> Dear Jim Brochu --
> I read the Irish piece and enjoyed it -- I frankly do not think in its present shape you'd have any chance in setting it up -- But it struck me that the characters might make a series -- I have one or two people I can send you to if you wish --
> As for myself -- I think I would be totally miscast and actually at the moment I'm not interested in doing a play --
>
> *Katharine Hepburn*

20th Century Fox optioned the property for $5000. I signed the contract and kept staring at this legal document where I signed my name right under Lucille Ball. I was supposed to get the check at the signing but Gary told me the money had been issued to Lucille Ball Productions and they would be paying me soon. Odd.

A few weeks later, Lucy and I were playing and she asked me jokingly if I had spent all my money from our project or invested it. I said I hadn't been paid yet. She looked at me and tilted her head. She didn't say anything more about it and we kept playing.

When I got home about three hours later, there was a message on my answering machine from Lucy (which I saved and still have) telling me I should go by the office the next morning and pick up my check. And so I did.

Lucy said that she always believed Gary was faithful, unlike Desi. She explained that Gary was on the golf course and she had no reason to worry or think about where else he might be.

But a few months after Lucy died, Gary married his golf pro, a lady named Susan, so Lucy might have known where Gary was but I don't think she knew exactly what he was doing. I think Gary Morton was one of the most avarice unfeeling uncaring users I've ever met in my life who forced Lucy to do things she didn't want to do so that he could have a job.

I couldn't believe I was sitting between Alice Kramden and Lucy Ricardo. Lucky boy.

Lucy was never able to do *The Lucky O'Learys* because of a series of small strokes which limited her physical ability and dulled her comic chops. Her health just didn't permit it. But getting the show produced was far less important than becoming Lucy's friend. Steve and I were honored to be included in her social circle and it was a privilege to sit at the dinner table with her.

She invited us to Thanksgiving at her home in Rancho Mirage. We had a backgammon tournament wedged between courses and Lucy and I got into a bout about lemonade. She used a sugar free mix and then added sweet and low which was like drinking chemicals. I told her it was too much. She said it wasn't. We started to raise our voices and finally Steve came in to see what all the yelling was about. Just before we left, Lucy took two lemons and placed them strategically for a photo with us.

I picked out her Oscar dress, a black, beaded slinky number with a gold collar that gave her legs great Southern exposure. The day after the ceremony, she left me a tongue-in-cheek message complaining about how damned heavy the dress was. But, God, she looked spectacular.

Three weeks before she died, she invited Steve and me to go see her daughter Lucie Arnaz perform at a benefit. When I got to the table, I read the place cards and saw my name next to Audrey Meadows, who she had wanted to play her sister in the *O'Learys*.

Audrey was a good old gal who smoked too much and laughed at everything anyone said. She was truly a lot of fun to be with. It was surreal for a child of the 50s to be sitting between Lucy Ricardo and Alice Kramden.

Backed up by Ronnie Abel and his orchestra, Lucie Arnaz was absolutely brilliant that night. Lucy once told me I was a born entertainer and the same is true for her daughter. She brought the house down. And deservedly so. Lucie Arnaz is the perfect blend of both parents inheriting the comedy timing of her mother and the musical chops of her dad, Desi. I took this picture of Lucy and Lucie right after the show and it might be the last one ever taken of the two of them. I don't know that for sure but Lucy was in the hospital a few weeks later.

My book about Lucy is a love-letter to the lady. She told me a lot of intimate stuff that could have burned the pages but I didn't include any of it. Nor will I here. *Lucy In The Afternoon* was a flattering portrait of a lady I loved.

I sent Lucie and Gary galleys of the book naively thinking it would please them. Morton called me the next day, screaming profanities and accusing me of using his wife to make a buck. (Something he had done for years.) He swore he was going to get revenge. Revenge? And then came the cliché I had often heard in the movies but never thought I would hear it applied to me. "You're through in show business," he thundered and hung up.

The first time I ran into Lucie Arnaz after writing the book was at a theater opening and she glared at me with a stare that would melt a thousand icebergs. She wasn't pleased that the book had come out so soon after her mother died. Truth is I never intended to write a book.

I had a friend in New York who would call me almost daily and ask, "What did Lucy talk about today?" I started to take notes so I would remember and then realized I had a book after she died. The story of her life as she told it to me over the backgammon table. It was my agent who suggested I write a book and made a deal with William Morrow after they read a sample chapter.

Over the years, Lucie Arnaz and I have developed a warm relationship and I don't think I can say enough wonderful things to describe this lady. Some children of celebrities are snobbish, entitled brats but Lucie is genuine, spiritual and embraces the light in all people.
She is a luminous entertainer as well as a devoted mother and wife. You don't read about her children involved in scandals because they are all very accomplished individuals. She's been married to her husband Larry Luckinbill forever and together they are truly the aristocracy of show business society. She's one of my heroes.

Since I was a kid I had always wanted Lucy's autograph and made two unsuccessful attempts to obtain it. I asked her once after seeing her on Broadway and another time after her comedy class in Hollywood. One day, Lucy and I were going through some of her scrapbooks which she kept in a small closet in the living room. It's where she kept all of her *I Love Lucy* scripts bound in leather.

She even found one of her Wildcat scripts (there were several I learned) and said to me, "Do you want this?" Yes, please. I thought her name would be on the front page but, although there were lots of notes on the pages, there was no signature.

About a year after Lucy died, we got a call from Steve's brother Scott in Texas. He was almost yelling into the phone, "Paul Harvey is talking about Jim on the radio. Paul Harvey is talking about Jim! On the radio!!!" We didn't think much of it. I had never met Paul Harvey and he didn't know me from Adam. When we listened to the rebroadcast, the story he told made me weep. Mr. Harvey tells this story better than I could. Paul Harvey said;

"Little Jimmy Brochu was thirteen years old and headed for the disappointment of his young life. He had just seen a Broadway play called Wildcat starring Lucille Ball. Now this was 1960. Lucy was Jimmy's favorite television star and seeing her in person had meant the world. How much more it would mean if only Jimmy could have Lucy's autograph.

So he hung around the theater until the audience had left and there in the back in the darkness Jimmy waited for a glimpse of his comic heroine, Sure enough, after what seemed a very long time, Lucille Ball herself appeared on the empty stage, walking casually across it in a flowing dressing gown.

Elated, Jimmy bounded down the aisle until he was standing at the Footlights looking up at the startled Lucy waving a theater program in his hand "Would you sign this please?" the boy asked? Lucy half-smiled back at him and said, "Sorry, no autographs today" and walked away.

But this is the rest of the story. Jimmy Brochu continued to adore Lucy anyway. In fact and at least partly because of her he sustained a love for show business, the theater in particular -comedy writing even more especially. You may recognize his name Brochu. His early passion to conjure laughter through words one day led Jim Brochu to Hollywood where eventually he realized his own dreams and where much to his joy he actually became friends with his childhood love Lucille Ball. I mean good friends. Such good friends that Jim often rearranged his writing schedule to leave his afternoons free for Lucy.

Her favorite game was backgammon. Jim and Lucy would sometimes spend hours at her backgammon board at twenty-five cents a point. Sometimes the two would just reminisce through Lucy's leather bound scrapbooks or just sit there at her dining room table going through photos - recent and distant – laughing. sometimes crying.

And then there was one that one occasion when Lucy left the room and she returned holding an eight by ten glossy of herself. Nobody knows why this happened on that particular day but she's carrying this photograph of herself. It was a studio publicity photograph from the 1940s. It was a glamorous pose. Lucy draped in white fur with her hair piled high. Thrusting this before Jim, she asked, "Have you ever seen this one?" Jim said no he hadn't but my it was lovely. Lucy said, "I'll put it by the door and later when you leave take it with you/" Then later when he left he did.

Now that was Monday, April 17th of this year (1989) Remaining to Lucille Ball were only a few hours of health and a few more hours to live. Oh, and did I mention the precious photo was signed this way, "Jim dear, You are very special, Love, Lucy." Jim Brochu, the thirteen-year old boy clutching a theater program eventually his heroine's friend and confidante had finally, but just in time, received from the great Lucille Ball her last autograph. And now you know the rest of the story."

After having my soul drained by the Disney organization I was dying to get back on stage. I read a casting notice in one of the local trade papers that Rue McClanahan had written a musical and they were having an open call at the Golden Theatre in Burbank.

The Golden was a very successful 99 seat theater that did a lot of original new musicals and they scheduled McClanahan's musical called *Oedipus, Schmedipus, As Long As You Love Your Mother* as their next production.

I had met Rue back in the 70s but there is no way she would have ever remembered me. I went to the open audition at the theatre where Rue, the director and the producer were running the call.

I sang my song, read the part and got a big "Thank you" from the director, a fella named Gregory Scott Young. I left the building and got about halfway across the street before the director came running out and told me to come back. They said they would like me to read some more and sing some more and sure enough I got the lead in *Oedipus, Schmedipus*. La McClanahan wrote the book, music and lyrics to a very cute show about ancient Greece which was an absolute rip off of *A Funny Thing Happened on the Way to the Forum* and I was playing Pseudolus. But in Rue's show he was called Eurasculus.

Rehearsals were fun but Rue wouldn't let the director direct. She gave the actors mountains of notes so that after a few shows her picky notes went in one ear and out the other. She would come backstage at intermission and give notes. Even during the last few performances. We had a turntable on stage and joked that Rue would revolve around one night in the middle of a show to give us notes.

Rue and I started to hang out during breaks and then went out for lunch and dinner together. She invited Steve and me to "Saturday Game Night" at her home in Encino. Her home was modern, on a gated sloping manicured hill and you were greeted at the door by a six-foot wooden carving of an African warrior complete with an erect, wooden, footlong African warrior penis. Rue was using it for a necklace rack.

There were about eight of us there on our first Game Night. Rue said, "Let's play Charades! You've played Charades before haven't you?" I told her I hadn't played Charades in twenty years and the last time was the most memorable, uncomfortable and embarrassing Charades game of my life.

It happened when I was performing at the Goodspeed Opera House and my friend Maureen Stapleton was at the neighboring Ivoryton Theater in Essex starring in *The Gingerbread Lady*. I knew Mo loved to play charades so after our shows one night I hosted a Charades Night for her. The whole cast would be there and were very excited to play with one of America's greatest living actresses

Charades Night at Goodspeed with Mo Stapleton and set designer Ray Kurtz. Why I'm on my knees is anybody's guess.

There was a young girl in the show named Sidney Blake who was so excited to meet Maureen Stapleton that she was having stomach pains. She just wanted to impress Ms. Stapleton and would do anything to please her. Mo arrived already a little on the tipsy side, in fact a lot on the tipsy side. We all had a couple of glasses of wine and Maureen picked out the teams for the games. Sydney and I were picked to be on Mo's team along with Lu Leonard and Gary Gage, two great character actors. Team Captain Maureen was giving us all the signals in the bedroom and Sidney was trying to remember as much as possible because she was so anxious to be good and win it for Mo.

We started the game and Mo was the first one up after another glass of white wine. Mo stood in front of our team, opened the paper with the clue and inadvertently staggered backwards. Sidney thought she had begun and yelled, "Drunk! Bombed! Alcoholic! *Long Day's Journey Into Night*! *The Lost Weekend*!" Mo just stared at her and said, "What the fuck are you talking about? I haven't started yet!"

Rue McClanahan's Saturday Game Nights became a regular event and Rue, Steve and I became rather close. For some reason she liked to stick her finger in my ear. It started during *Oedipus Schmedipus* when one day she was checking the bows on my head piece and stuck her finger in my ear. After I had lost a great deal of weight about ten years later, I asked her to stick her finger in my ear again. I guess some people have a stick your finger in your ear fetish.

Rue, Steve and I were back in New York in the late 90s when she told me she had fallen in love and was going to marry someone who I actually had worked with during the 1970s. I told her as long as she was happy that I would support her in any way possible. About two weeks before the wedding, which was going to be held at the Waldorf Astoria, I was at their apartment very early in the morning. I told her I was very upset because I had not gotten an invitation. She said, "Well, they haven't gone out yet."

I couldn't believe the wedding was two weeks away and the invitations hadn't been sent out. I said, "Where are they?" She said, "In the box in the kitchen waiting to get addressed and stamped." So we sat down for the rest of the day, addressed envelopes, licked stamps and sent out a hundred and fifty invites.

When the day of the wedding came we were to go to a certain secret apartment in the Waldorf Towers. Steve was in California so I took my friend Michael Alden. We gave the secret code to the concierge who pointed us to the elevator with the apartment number written on a piece of paper.

We got up to the floor and there was an empty coat rack outside the apartment door. We knocked on the door and it opened a crack. A Filipino man in a white servant's jacket asked what we wanted as a Filipino lady ran behind him into another room. "What do you want?" he demanded.

"We're here for the McClanahan-Wilson wedding?

"No wedding here," he barked. "Go away."

We went back downstairs to the lobby and another concierge told us the wedding had been moved to a different apartment. We finally got to the right suite as the ceremony was about to begin. Rue looked at me and said, "Oh good. Thank God you're here. At least I'll know a few people." I asked what happened to the other suite. She said, "Well, that was Imelda Marcos' apartment and she came back last night."

At the beginning of 1993 Steve wasn't feeling well. He had symptoms that were scaring us and so we both decided to get tested for AIDS. We went to the testing center on Vineland Blvd, took the test and a few days later we went back for the results. We both were taken into different rooms to speak with the nurses. My nurse told me I tested negative and my whole session with her lasted less than five minutes. I went out to the street and waited for Steve thinking he would also be out in a minute.

As the time stretched into fifteen minutes, then twenty, I knew. When he came out a half hour later, he didn't have to say anything. The look on his face told me everything. We stood on the street, embraced each other and wept. He had just received a death sentence.

CHAPTER TEN
Lemonade from Lemons

The Zephyr Theatre production of *The Last Session* with Francesca P. Roberts, Marjory Graue, Steve, Doug "The Greaseman" Tracht and Charles Esten.

About a year after his initial diagnosis, Steve had developed full-blown AIDS and was critically ill. In all that time, he had never uttered the word, "AIDS" out loud.

It was Mother's Day May 8, 1994 and Steve was lying on the couch barely able to breathe. So I picked him up, threw him in the car, took him to the Emergency Room at Santa Monica Hospital. It wasn't difficult because he only had about one hundred and thirty pounds on his six-foot-two frame.

When we got to the emergency room it was very crowded and the only place for Steve was on a gurney in the hallway. All of a sudden Anson Williams, Potsie from *Happy Days*, appeared. His wife had choked on a chicken bone and they came to Santa Monica hospital to make sure she was OK. Williams saw Steve lying on the gurney and said and the most cheerful way, "Well, hi!"

Steve said, "Hi."

"Well, how are you?" he asked.

Steve could barely say, "Not good."

Anson said, "Well, what's the matter with you?"

Suddenly, Steve sat bolt upright on the and screamed at the top of his breath, "I HAVE AIDS!"

Bedpans dropped, curtains flew open and nurses turned around. Anson Williams came over to the gurney and took Steve's hand. He said, "Well you're not going to die today. You still have plenty of life left in you so keep a positive attitude because you still have a lot of things you have left to do. Okay?" And with that he shook Steve's hand and was gone. We joked that Steve decided to live that day because he didn't want the last celebrity he ever saw in his life to be Potsie.

Steve was in the hospital for two months. A few days after he came home, he said, "I have to play something for you." He sat down at the piano and played a song he had written called "Connected." He had given up his own music career to work for other songwriters so it had been years since he had written the song. "Connected" was about his experience in the hospital.

"I saw a neon sign that said "emergency."
I barely even knew what happened next.

Collapsing in the doorway and then down the hall, connected to a meter. We should all be connected to a meter."

He only played about eight bars before we both started crying. When we collected ourselves he played the whole song and it was absolutely brilliant; truly one of the greatest songs I had ever heard in my life. Thirty-two bars of heart and soul on a music staff. And he was coming back to life through his work.

I saw the effect the creative process was having on him and so I started giving him homework assignments. I told him to write a song about the group he went to or how people say they have a cure for AIDS but that nobody can find the people who said they had it. I told him to write a song about his own memorial service.

One by one he wrote ten meaningful, tuneful songs and was worried they were going to die with him. He said, "You're a playwright. Why don't you write a play and put the songs in it?" It was a wonderful challenge.

It stuck me that I really didn't have a clue what to do until Thanksgiving. I knew I wanted to write a play about the Christian vs. Gay conflict but had no idea of the characters or plot. We were at a friend's house who had a recording studio in his garage. After dinner, Steve sat down at the keyboard and started to play his songs and a couple of the other guests who were singers started to pick up the beat and sing along with him. And bang! I saw the whole show. The idea was given to me in what I can only call a flash of grace. I literally saw the whole play and all the characters. I sat down to write it and within a week the first draft was finished. We called it *Gideon's Bible*. In the second draft, the show became *The Last Session*.

Steve had met a lot of wonderful people when he was working for the Songwriters Association, especially at ASCAP. His health problems had affected our finances and the medical bills were piling up. Lorena Munoz, who was the head of ASCAP, asked if they could sponsor a benefit to raise money for Steve's health care. They suggested that we present a reading of the new musical we had just written. It was to be done at the Cinegrill at the Hollywood Roosevelt Hotel.

We asked Rue McClanahan if she would host the event and she actually got out of a sick bed with a one hundred and two degree temperature to come to the Cinegrill to do this for us. I'll never forget her for that.

What happened that night was so extraordinary that I can't even adequately put it into words. People were overwhelmed by Steve's score and I knew the book was not great but had "good bones" and I could develop it.

Around this time, two Angels came into our lives. I use that term not only because they were "theatrical' angels that backed the show, but they were true earthly angels who brought love and light to whatever they touched, Kim and Ronda Espy.

Kim and Ronda owned a publishing business called Bob-A-Lew Music and they came to the Cinegrill presentation. Ronda, who was a member of the Board of Directors of ASCAP, was especially moved by the music and the message of the show and she optioned *The Last Session* for a New York production.

Steve with Ronda and Kim Espy, two angels in every sense of the word.

Before the show could go anywhere, we needed to do a workshop production so I could really get under the hood and fix the book. Our friend Eleanor Albano suggest we check out the Zephyr Theater in Hollywood because they did readings and workshops of new plays and musicals.

Into our lives came two more angels; Gary Guidinger and Linda Toliver, producers of the Zephyr Theatre. They were working on the stage when we came in unannounced and introduced ourselves. Our first impression was that they were two creative, generous spirits who loved each other and the theatre. We were right.

We told them about *The Last Session* and they were interested in hearing more. We wanted to leave them the script and a tape of the music then Gary said, "You know we do a series of readings on Saturday afternoons and the one we had for this Saturday just fell out. Do you think you could do your show then?"

This was on a Wednesday and they wanted it by Saturday. We called the actors who had done The Cinegrill reading for us and they were all available. In three days we pulled together a performance that was so successful that Gary and Linda offered to produce a workshop of the show on the spot. They believed in the message of the show and wanted to be the first to produce it. And unlike many other producers, they asked for no financial participation in future productions.

The actors who had performed The Cinegrill reading were darling friends who were excellent singers but now we needed excellent actors. We were lucky to get Francesca P. Roberts as Tryshia, Marjory Graue as Vicki, Doug Tracht who was a big radio star nicknamed "The Greaseman," as Jim and Charles Esten as Buddy. Charles, who we affectionately call Chip, has gone on to huge success in television and music as the star of many TV shows including *Nashville and Who's Line Is It Anyway?* A truly remarkable, talented and wonderful man.

Steve was to play Gideon but was still so ill that he was being fed by an intravenous tube twenty-four hours a day. I had to disconnect it before he went on stage every night. His parents came from Arkansas to see the show. At the end I said to his mother, "Did you like it?" She said, "Yes. I just wish it was about somebody else."

I shouldn't have pushed but said, "Did you have a favorite part?"

She said, "Oh, yes. The seating arrangements."

The show was taking on new life but sadly Steve was still dying. Everything we were doing was "the last." The last birthday. The last trip. The last Thanksgiving. The last Christmas...and then a miracle happened/ A young doctor in Philadelphia named Bruce Dorsey was working for the Merck organization and was developing a cure for AIDS. He synthesized a drug called Crixivan which was having a tremendously positive effect on some trial patients. But the new miracle drug was very scarce and you could only get it by winning a medical lottery. His doctor, Ellie Goldstein, entered his name and Steve was one of the fortunate ones who received it. Within two weeks of taking it, we saw the change. He was beginning to gain weight. He had more energy and he was on the road to recovery.

A few months later, Steve was keeping a diary on the Internet. In fact, he was one of the web's very first bloggers beginning in June 1996. Doctor Dorsey read his blog and contacted Steve. He wrote, "You know, here in the laboratory I don't always see the effects my work has and I am so happy for all that has happened for you. Glad I could be a small part of it." A small part? Dr. Bruce Dorsey has saved thousands of lives through his research and was our honored guest at the opening night of *The Last Session* in New York. If it weren't for him, there would be no Steve to write it.

After another backers' audition in New York, presented by Kim and Ronda Espy, Carl D. White, who produced all the shows at the Golden Theatre, joined the team. Recasting the role of Gideon was going to be the greatest challenge because we needed a thin, sensational actor about forty years old who had a dynamite voice and played a helluva piano.

Then another prayer was answered when Bob Stillman walked it, sat at the piano and accompanied himself to a brilliant rendition of Edgar Winters' *Dying to Live*. (An amazingly appropriate choice.) He knocked us out of our seats and we had our leading man.

The Last Session opened at the 47th Street Theater on October 17, 1997, just eighteen months after the first reading at the Cinegrill - lightning speed for a musical to go from page to stage. Joining Bob Stillman was Amy Coleman (channeling Janis Joplin) as Vicki, Grace Garland as Tryshia, Dean Bradshaw as Jim and a magnificent Stephen Bienskie as the young Christian antagonist, Buddy.

The reviews were uniformly positive but people really weren't interested in seeing a musical about AIDS. Still, despite the topic, the show was so life affirming and entertaining that we ran for nine months. The producers of the Laguna Playhouse in California saw the show in New York and booked it for their theater a few months later. To me, the Laguna production was the ultimate perfect production of *The Last Session*. It boasted most of the New York cast with the addition of Michele "Maisey" Mais as Tryshia, who stopped the show every night with "The Singer and The Song."

The L.A. reviews were spectacular, even better than New York. Michael Alden, one of the producers of the New York production along with Ronda and Kim transferred the show to the Tiffany Theatre in Hollywood where the show ran for another six months. In 1998, *The Last Session* won the Los Angeles Drama Critics Circle Awards for Best Book, Best Music, Best Lyrics and Best Musical and the GLAAD Media Award for Best Theatre Show presented to us by David Hyde Pierce.

Over the years, *The Last Session* has been performed all over the United States. In 2012, the show was given a London production with one of England's brightest stars, Darren Day, as Gideon. We flew over for the rehearsals and the opening. It was very emotional to think about Steve coming back from the edge of death to see his work performed on the London stage. Happily, the show got rave reviews and an original London cast album was recorded.

"Exquisite! Exuberant!"
—Peter Marks, New York Times

"Superb! Bright & Funny!"
—Clive Barnes, New York Post

"Brilliant! Inspiring! Soaring!"
—John Heilpern, The New York Observer

"The 47th Street ROCKS to its Foundation!"
—In Theater

"A Sleeper Hit of A Musical! Don't Miss This One!"
—Liz Smith

But the New York production was not without a tremendous amount of pain. Shortly after the show opened, Steve and I broke up. For eighty days. All the pressure of the last couple of years was taking its toll. I was drinking too much. And there was an evil man connected with the show who had fallen in love with Steve and decided to break us up. He almost succeeded. But we realized that we had too much going for us to let that little shit get between us. As Anson Williams said, "We still had a lot of things left to do."

Speaking of Anson, a funny thing happened during the run of *The Last Session* in L.A. Steve was going to give a special concert talking about the show and how the songs were written. I told him to make sure to tell the Anson Williams story. What I didn't tell him was our producer had called Anson Williams and invited him to be in the audience. Anson and his wife we're thrilled to be there. He remembered the incident at Santa Monica Hospital as much as we did. He sat in the back of the audience until it was time for the surprise.

It took Steve a few seconds to realize that Anson Williams had surprised him.

Steve got to the point of the evening where he was about to sing "Connected." He began to tell the Anson story and I gave Anson the cue to go onstage. Steve looked up, saw him and had absolutely no idea who the hell it was. It took him about five seconds to realize that it was Anson Williams. Anson told the audience how deeply the encounter with Steve at the hospital had affected him as well.

About a year after *The Last Session* played the Laguna Playhouse, we got a call from Rick Stein, the theatre's Executive Director. He told us that they were doing a series of special events and wanted us to appear in one of them. We didn't have anything like that put together and I asked Rick what he thought we should do?" He said, "Talk about how you created *The Last Session*, sing a few songs, tell a few stories…you know. Just improvise."

I have never been able to improvise in my life so I sat down and wrote a book around some of Steve's new songs. One thing that Steve and I had in common was we both almost went into the Church business: me as a Catholic priest and him as a Baptist preacher. We also believed that show business and religion were two sides of the same coin. So we called the new show "The Big Voice: God or Merman?" and took our new show to Laguna Beach. We played to a standing-room only crowd and their reaction was off the chart. The show ran ten minutes over just because of the laughs and applause that were added. Then, we worked on the show by taking it on the road playing San Francisco, Rochester, Philadelphia, Chicago, Omaha, Houston and Dallas.

We loved the way some of the reviews tried to characterize our relationship. Our favorite was from the San Francisco Chronicle which said, "Picture

With Ethel Merman's son Bob Levitt

Anthony Perkins and Orson Welles in love." When we played Dallas, Steve's brother Corky who lived there called us early in the morning and said "You'd better get the *Dallas Morning News*. There's a little article about your little show." We ran out to get the paper and found we were the whole 'above the fold" article with the headline "Divine Inspiration."

During our San Francisco run, Ethel Merman's son, Bob Levitt, came to see us. Bob and I knew each other slightly from Carnegie Tech but I hadn't seen him in years. He knew I had known his mom and grandparents. In fact he told me his mom had saved a letter I had sent her years before. It was a very emotional meeting. He was very touched by our tribute to his mother and gave his blessing to the show.

Then two of our *Last Session* angels, Gary Guidinger and Linda Toliver, invited us to do a run of the show back at the Zephyr Theatre in Hollywood. They hired a young man named Jeramiah Peay to stage manage and our bond became so great that he has stage managed every show of mine since then.

After some rewrites and a few new songs, we opened on October 29, 2002 for a three week run. Instead, the show ran for twelve weeks and won the Los Angeles Stage Ovation Award (the L.A. version of the Tony) for Best Musical presented to us by Jerry Herman.

It was such a thrill to go on that stage and have that award handed to us by the man who wrote *Hello, Dolly!* - the show where I sold orange drinks as a kid.

A few months later, a producer friend named Ed Gaynes called and said that The Actors' Temple in New York City, a celebrated synagogue for "theatricals" was being transformed into a 200 seat Off-Broadway theater. Were we interested in being the first show to play there? *The Big Voice: God or Merman?* opened Off-Broadway at the Actors' Temple Theater on November 30, 2006.

That night after the show opened we were in our apartment in New York waiting for the New York *Times* review. When it came out we were absolutely flabbergasted, looking for the negatives, but they never came. It was the greatest review we've ever gotten. And from *The New York Times*; "Side-splitting, touching and triumphant...a hilarious and utterly enthralling evening of musical theatre."

The Big Voice ran six months and since Steve and I had other commitments, two other actors replaced us. It was like watching somebody else use your toothbrush. Dale Radunz played me and Carl Danielson played Steve. They might have been better than we were.

During our New York run of *The Big Voice*, we got a beautiful letter from Tony Cointreau who was the executor of the Merman estate. He invited Steve and me up to his apartment where he had collected a treasure trove of Ethel's memorabilia. After about an hour of reminiscing about 'the Merm," Tony left the room and returned with the urn containing Ethel's ashes. He put them in my arms and I got very emotional holding her once again. Oh, and her urn was made of pure brass. How appropriate.

MURPHY CROSS & PAUL KREPPEL
BEST MUSICAL 2005
L.A. STAGE OVATION AWARD
THE BIG VOICE
GOD OR MERMAN?
BEST MUSICAL
BEST MUSICAL
BEST WRITING
BEST SCORE
BEST ACTOR
JIM BROCHU
VALLEY THEATRE LEAGUE AWARD
PALM SPRINGS DESERT STAR AWARD
"Priceless, Witty & Inspiring!"
"Potent & Provocative!"
"Hilarious & Heartbreaking!"
"Absolutely Tremendous!"
"Riotously entertaining!"
"Theatrical Dynamite!"
A MUSICAL COMEDY IN TWO LIVES
Written and Performed by
Steve SCHALCHLIN Jim BROCHU
Directed by
Anthony BARNAO
THE ACTORS TEMPLE THEATRE
339 West 47th Street
Tickets available at TELECHARGE 212-239-6200
www.thebigvoice.com

CHAPTER ELEVEN
Zero Attraction

I was doing Zero when I was eighteen.

The picture above is from my 1964 high school yearbook. It states that I was known as the "Zero Mostel" of LaSalle. The writer predicts I would become and actor and a writer. Almost fifty years later, those three elements of Zero, acting and writing would combine to produce one of the greatest experiences of my life, theatrical or otherwise.

The night I saw *A Funny Thing Happened on the Way to the Forum* I had no idea who or what a Zero Mostel was. And yet when he burst through the curtains I could feel myself being pushed back in the seat like somebody had stepped on the accelerator and a force of nature was thrusting me backwards. Here was this big man, so light on his feet…screaming, making faces and everything he did was just plain hilarious…one of the most astonishing performances I had ever seen.

From the time I was in high school I had always been compared to Zero Mostel. My girth and desire to get a laugh helped the comparison. Then I nursed it along by studying his mannerisms and delivery. I even went on to play some of his iconic roles like Pseudolus and Tevye.

It was while we were doing *The Big Voice* that I started to think seriously about writing a one man show about Zero. Zero was sixty-two years old when he died and I was fast approaching that age so if I were going to do it now was the time.

But then of course fate intervened and I took a little detour. When we were doing *The Last Session* at the 47th Street Theater, a man named Geoff Shlaes was the executive director. In 1999, I had heard he had taken over as producer of the El Portal Theater in North Hollywood, which was just a few blocks from our house. One afternoon, Steve and I stopped by to say hello, welcome him to the neighborhood and congratulate him on the new job.

He gave us a tour of the theater, a 1926 movie palace that had been destroyed in the Northridge Earthquake. Steve and I experienced that frightening earthquake firsthand. It was 4:30 in the morning on January 17, 1994 and I had actually just gotten up to go to the bathroom. When I came back to bed, it hit. It started with a tremendous jolt. The whole place began to shake and it seemed like it would never stop.

Steve and I grabbed each other. We were both terrified. That rolling and shaking went on for almost a minute and when it stopped, we tried to see the damage but it was still dark and the power was gone. With the first light, we saw everything had come off the walls, the bookcases were turned over, the television on the floor and lamps smashed. We were lucky that the whole house didn't cave in on top of us.

The next day we drove around and saw much of our neighborhood had been destroyed, including my bank which was now in pieces on the ground. But the El Portal Theatre was really hurt and then a group of actors got together to save and renovate it.

The plan was to turn the twelve hundred seat theater into three separate theaters with four hundred seats, ninety-nine seats and fifty seats. It was truly a three ring circus. Geoff was happy to see us but said he couldn't spend much time with us because he was looking for someone to write and direct the first show in the new theatre – a benefit to honor Donald O'Connor and dedicate the theater. Then Geoff looked at me and said, "Oh my God! I think I'm looking for you. Do you wanna write and direct it?" I said, "Absolutely." He said, "We'd like it to open with a big splash and have a star-studded performance. Do you know any stars?" I told him I was friends with several names but they were still my friends because I had never called to ask a favor from any of them. But I said, "I will for this."

So I called all the great people that I thought would make a wonderful show and they all said yes: Carol Channing Edie Adams, Doris Roberts Kathleen Freeman, Rip Taylor, Gary Marshall and Jo Anne Worley and the legendary Fayard Nicholas of The Nicholas Brothers. There were endless speeches before the show concluding with our Congressman, Howard Berman. He made me laugh when he began his remarks with "Everything that can be said has been said it's just that not everyone has said it."

The benefit was an enormous success but for some reason Geoff got fired and shortly after I was asked to come back as Artistic Director of the El Portal. One of the shows I always wanted to do was *70, Girls, 70*. I had always loved the show so much and felt I could give it another life by rewriting the book and moving some songs around.

I got in touch with John Kander and Fred Ebb who gave me permission to do it and I cast Charlotte Rae, Mrs. Garrett from *The Facts Of Life* in the lead role of Ida. Rounding out the cast was a troupe of veterans: Jane Kean, Marni Nixon, William Schallert and Robert Mandan. Fred Ebb came out to work with me on the script. Fred was not in good condition. We went to lunch and he tried to eat his bowl of spaghetti but his hand was shaking so much he could hardly bring it up to his mouth.

Every idea I gave Fred, he shot down. But at the end of the meeting, he said, "I like that you have ideas and I love that you love the show. But it is what it is and will stay what it is."

Although Charlotte became a dear friend of ours eventually, I made a big mistake by casting her in the lead. She absolutely destroyed the show by making it all about herself. She wanted everybody else's lines, everybody else's songs and then when I capitulated to her wants, she couldn't deliver the goods. She couldn't remember lines or blocking and was more interested in giving the other actors notes which made for a tense atmosphere and hurt the show tremendously.

At one point she refused to do a song that was in the show so I called John Kander and asked him for guidance. He was very sweet and understanding. John said, "OK, Fred and I have a brand new song that she may like better." A few minutes later the fax machine started whirring and out came a song called, "I Move On."

Steve was the first person to play it. It was a charming song, not as good as "The Elephant Song" which she wanted cut. Charlotte didn't like the new song either and so I cut the scene. "I Move On" didn't go to waste because a few years later they put it into the film of *Chicago*.

Our *70 girls 70* was not a success. The book still didn't work and having Charlotte in the lead dragged the whole process down. The reviews were uniformly terrible but at least I gave it a shot, though not successfully. I love *70, Girls, 70* and I will always love *70, Girls, 70* and in fact a few years ago I got to play Davy's part of Harry at a concert at Feinstein's nightclub in New York. If you haven't heard the score, take a listen. It's one of Kander and Ebb's best.

The El Portal Theatre was starting to get off the ground and we were selling season subscriptions. But then came September 11th, 2001, the opening night of the first show of the season, *The Last of Mrs. Lincoln* by James

Prideaux starring Marcia Rodd. It was the story of Mary Lincoln's years after she left the White House and descended into madness.

The play was staged on a fifty-foot Civil War tattered American flag that hung from the back wall, covered the stage and draped into the orchestra pit. The country had been attacked and here we were literally walking all over the American flag.

I had to make the decision to cancel the show or go forward with the performance. I called the cast together and they all wanted me to cancel. But I decided that people needed a place to go. To escape the horror for a few hours.

I remembered the opening scene from the film of *The Dresser*. As Albert Finney is walking through the streets of a devastated war-torn London, he sees a woman sitting in the rubble. He takes two tickets from his pocket and hands them to the woman. He says, "These are tickets for the theater tonight. I hope you will find comfort there." Just as I hoped our audience would find comfort in *our* theater. And they did.

The theater was absolutely packed that night. People just needed to get away. But the World Trade Center catastrophe affected ticket sales and future subscriptions. People were frightened of the future and they weren't about to spend money on a subscription. It hurt all the theaters in the country but ours in particular. So I was out of the job I didn't want in the first place.

After leaving the El Portal, I knew it was time to concentrate on the show about Zero. I read everything I could get my hands on and talked to most of his friends that I could find. He was a very complicated man who overcame so many obstacles and adversities that it was grist for a good play.

Zero was a Jew who was disowned by his family because he married a shicksa. He was blacklisted for being a communist in the 50s. And just as his career was starting to reignite, he was hit by a New York City bus and almost lost his left leg.

He had fifteen operations and spent six months in the hospital. One night after Forum, I was in his dressing room and he was wearing a blue terrycloth robe. The leg wasn't pretty. Zero used to say, "My left leg looks like chopped liver." He walked with a cane and was in constant pain on stage which is ironic when you think about all the laughter he was bringing to his audiences.

It took only a week to write the first draft of the play. At first I was going to call the show *Absolute Zero* so I would get a first place in the theatre listings. Then I read a story about Burgess Meredith directing Zero in James Joyce's *Ulysses in Nighttown*. Meredith said that Zero would get so loud in rehearsals that the walls of the old theatre would shake and Meredith would warn the cast, "Hold on to your tits everybody, it's Zero Hour!"

Though I knew I didn't have to get permission from the estate to write the play because Zero was a public figure. But I did want the family to know what I was doing. I found Josh Mostel's email address and I sent him a copy of the script, adding, "I'd love to know what you think."

Josh wrote back saying he didn't think anybody could pull off playing his father but as far as the script was concerned he had two corrections. I had used the word "capiche" which he said his father never would have used and I had spelled the playwright "Plautus" name wrong. Other than that it was historically correct.

Zero considered himself an artist who just did acting so he could buy more paint. So I set the play in his artist studio on West 28th St. and the conceit was he was giving an interview to an unseen reporter from the New York Times. When I finished the first draft, I needed to hear the play out loud in front of some people. Audiences tell you so much. And so Linda Fuller at the Avery Schreiber Theater in North Hollywood offered her venue for a reading.

I was at a cocktail party a few days before and was inviting a friend to come see it. Another man, standing close by turned to me and said. "Did I just hear you say you were doing a play about Zero Mostel?

I told him I was and he introduced himself as Herb Isaacs, the Artistic Director of the West Coast Jewish Theater. Could he come? Sure.

I asked my friend Piper Laurie if she would come see it and afterward she had so many wonderful ideas that I eventually asked her to direct the piece. Piper, or Rosie as her friends call her, isn't the kind of director who could do tech and lighting and blocking and things like that but she was brilliant about editing the text, finding the arc of the show and making the most out of the best dramatic moments.

At the intermission of the reading, the Artistic Director of the West Coast Jewish Theatre offered a full production. I said, "But you haven't seen act two." He said he didn't have to.

Zero Hour opened at the

Egyptian Studio Theater in Hollywood on July 7, 2006. We were supposed to run three weeks, then the three week run was extended to twelve weeks. When the L.A. Ovation Awards were announced for that year, I was nominated for three and won for Best New Play presented to me by my pal, David Hyde Pierce. During the L.A. run of the show, many of Zero's friends came to see the piece and it made me nervous. A some of them were coming to see my performance but also some of them were coming to judge. They were all very fond of Zero and were coming out of a sense of protection.

    I was most nervous when I heard Theodore Bikel was coming. He and Zero were very close and I could see him sitting in the third row. I was hoping he would come back and tell me what he thought but he disappeared after and I was left thinking he hated the play and hated me.

    Two Days Later this letter arrived.

Dear Jim (if I may):

My wife Tamara and I saw your play last night and I wanted to tell you how very impressed I was with both the performance and the writing.

You probably know Zero and I knew each other quite well, saw each other from time to time and chatted mostly in Yiddish.

Several months after Zee's death I was chatting with Madeline Lee Gilford and as usual we talked about Zero - About his irrepressible nature, about how no stage had been large enough to contain him and how outrageous he had been on and off stage. Then I remember Madeline saying, "I don't know where he is now but wherever he is they've already asked him to leave."

I was particularly moved by the way you dealt with the moments about Phil Loeb. Rather than breaking down as so many actors might have been tempted to do, you danced on the edge of a breakdown. It was a great and wonderful feat of acting. Your writing also impressed me greatly; it captured the nuances of Zee's personality and solved the tricky problems that always attended a one man performance.

After Rhinoceros opened a friend of mine who had seen it ran into Lee J Cobb and said to him, "Lee you must see Zero in this play. I'm telling you that without the aid of make up the man turns into a roaring, charging rhinoceros. Lee Cobb said, " I have yet to see him in a play where he didn't!"

Once again let me thank you for having brought back to us the memory of a volcano that was thought to be long extinct.

Best regards, Theo Bikel

That letter meant the world to me. When the show was nominated for the Drama Desk in New York, sadly Theo was my competition for his own one man show

Rehearsing with Theo Bikel for The Sunshine Boys at Theatre J in Washington, DC

about Sholem Aleichem.. After I won, he embraced me in a bear hug and said, "Well, deserved, my friend. Well done. Now, let's do *The Sunshine Boys* together. And that actually happened.

Theo and I went to DC to do a benefit for Theatre J with me as Willie and Theo as Al. Such a thrill to work with such a gifted actor.

Kenn McLoughlin, the Artistic Director of Stages Repertory Theatre in Houston, where we had done *The Big Voice,* asked me to come back with the new show. Then it was up to San Francisco for a few months to do a run at Ed Decker's New Conservatory Theater Center. So once again I was on the road trying out a new show.

Then after Chicago, San Diego, Rochester, Tucson and Miami (where I won the Carbonell Award as Best Actor) it was time to take the show to New York. *Zero Hour* was optioned by two New York producers, Kurt Peterson and Ed Gaynes, but before the New York run we were given a final "try out" production by Ari Roth at Theater J in Washington DC.

Once again the reviews were uniformly positive and we had the money to go to New York. My best friend Rich Bloch lived in Washington and was at the show almost every night. Rich and Sue Bloch, beside from being genetically kind and smart, are two of the most interesting people in the country.

In 2004, Rich and I were working on a cruise ship when we met. He was there to do his magic act and his wife Sue was there to be his assistant and hold the magical flowering pot tray. What I only learned later was that he is one of the country's foremost arbitrators as well as one of the country's top magicians. He has presided over the settlements of some very major labor disputes. And his wife Sue, the magical flower pot holder, is a

Constitutional Law Professor at Georgetown University and a Supreme Court historian and scholar. She was also Thurgood Marshall's law clerk.

Rich was driving Steve and me to his house for dinner on the night off when the lead producer call to say an investor pulled out and we didn't have the money to open. I was shaken when I hung up. I told them what happened and Rich calmly asked, "How much do you need?" I told him the figure which was not a small amount. All he said was, "I've got your back." Now with the name Richard I. Bloch added to the producing team, we opened Off-Broadway at the Theatre at St. Clements on November 14, 2009 and ran for over 400 performances. It was where I had made my Off-Broadway debut in *Endicott and the Red Cross* forty-two years previously. Talk about coming full circle.

The show garnered all the major theatre nominations that year with the biggest prize being the New York Drama Desk Award which included Broadway and Off-Broadway productions. I was up for Best Solo Show opposite some real heavyweights including Carrie Fisher, Anna Deavere-Smith, Judith Ivey, Coleman Domingo and Theodore Bikel. I felt like I had been nominated for best supporting solo show.

Then came the night of the awards and I kept my fingers crossed. At least it would be a fun night out. The ceremony began with the ageless Mitzi Gaynor giving an award. followed by Martha Plimpton who said, "Mitzi Gaynor just told me she loved my shoes. Who needs drugs?" Matthew Modine was the next presenter and he said, "Mitzi Gaynor just told me she loved my underwear. Who needs drugs?"

My category was next and Ana Gasteyer announced my name. "The winner is Jim Brochu!" I came to the mic and I said, "Funny, Mitzi Gaynor just told me to go fuck myself." The place exploded. Ana Gasteyer doubled over and the producers of the event told me I had gotten the longest laugh in the history of the Drama Desk.

That year, I was also nominated for the Washington, DC Helen Hayes Award for Best Actor in a play. Steve and I went to Washington and joined our friends Rich and Sue Bloch, for the ceremony.

Edward Albee and Terrence McNally were watching me from the wings.

The big breeze

that flew into Washington that year was an Australian production of *A Streetcar Named Desire* starring Cate Blanchett. I was up against the fellow playing Stanley Kowalski who seemed to have the buzz. The moment came for the big awards. Cate Blanchett won Best Actress and I won Best Actor. Then came one of the most memorable moments of my life.

I accepted the award, thanked the audience and headed to the wings. I wasn't wearing my glasses and so all I saw were two blurred, shadowy figures standing in the wings. They were the next presenters waiting to go on. They both stretched out their arms and we embraced in the three way hug. It was only when I got next to them did I realize I was having a three-way hug with Edward Albee and Terrence McNally, two of America's greatest living playwrights.

Terrence said he wanted to come see *Zero Hour* when he got back to New York and sure enough two nights later Terrence McNally was in the audience with his husband producer Tom Kirdahy.

Steve and I with three of the giants of Broadway; Sheldon Harnick, Jerry Bock and Barbara Cook.

When *Zero Hour* opened in New York, Steve and I were still living in LA but we knew where our hearts were and decided to move back to New York City. Steve closed up the apartment, sold stuff, gave stuff away, dumped other stuff and he did it all by himself. My hero.

One of the greatest joys in my life came during the run of Zero Hour in New York. Sheldon Harnick and Jerry Bock, the composers of *Fiddler on the Roof* were receiving the Oscar Hammerstein Lifetime Achievement Award. The producer, Jim Morgan, asked me to sing "If I Were A Rich Man."

It was surreal to look down and see all the creators of *Fiddler* looking back: Hal Prince, Joe Stein (who wrote the book) and of course, Bock and Harnick. I was the penultimate act and the closer was Barbara Cook who sang a thrilling A Capella "Till Tomorrow" from *Fiorello*.

I usually don't get nervous before a performance. Excited yes, nervous no. But when Marion Seldes called and asked me for *Zero Hour* tickets, I got very nervous. How often do you perform in front of the First Lady of the American Theater?

Marion played Zero Mostel's daughter in *The Merchant*, the play he did one performance of in Philadelphia and then died. She told me she was crazy about Zero and I think part of her wanting to see the show was not only to support me, but to be critical of how I could pull it off.

I was very aware she was in the house and I pretty much played the whole show to her. I went back to my dressing room and thought about how often I had gone backstage to see Marion after a show. It was heady to think she was coming back to see me. I quickly washed my face, combed my hair back and waited for the great

Seldes to appear. The door to the backstage area opened and there she was.

Marion Seldes didn't think I was horrible.

Marion had her head down and was shaking it back and forth, repeating over and over again "Horrible. It was just horrible. Horrible!" I panicked. I thought, "Oh my God, I'm going to get the worst review of my life from one of the greatest actresses of our time. But when she got closer to me she raised her head, embraced me and repeated, "Just horrible." I said, "Marion, was I really horrible?" "Oh, darling. No! You were brilliant. I thought I was watching Zero. But what they did to those poor people back in the blacklist days was just horrible. Horrible!" A few months after she saw the show, Marion was given a special Tony Award for Lifetime Achievement. Steve and I were watching at home when she came to the stage, accepted the award, nodded, clutched the award to her chest and walked off without saying a word. We were with her the next night and I asked her why she did what she did. She said when she got to the ceremony all the producers, one by one, came to her and said, "Keep it short. Keep it short. Keep it short!"

"So," she said, "I decided to keep it the shortest of anybody who's ever spoken." Her acceptance speech took a second. I hope the producers were happy. I know Marion was.

I took a hiatus from the New York production to bring the show to Toronto. I was picked up at the airport by the producer who said, "Josh Mostel is coming tomorrow night."

I was gobsmacked. "To see the show?" I asked.

"No, he is coming for the exhibit."

I learned that the theatre was having an exhibit of twenty of Zero's paintings in the lobby of the theater and Josh was coming up to open the exhibit. The producer said that Josh had made it very clear that he wouldn't see the show but would be happy to do some joint television interviews with me.

The morning of the opening, a taxi pulled up in front of my hotel with Josh Mostel almost filling the backseat. Josh reached out his hand and said, "I'm not seeing the show tonight." I told him was perfectly fine I understood that it must be an uncomfortable feeling to see some schmuck try to play his father.

During those four interviews Josh and I bonded. He told me stories about living through the blacklist with FBI men harassing them at home. He grew up afraid. Josh is a sweet, darling and super intelligent guy. After our three hour lunch I took him back to his hotel. As he was getting out of the car he turned to me, shook my hand and said, "I'm seeing the show tonight!" And sure enough, there was Josh sitting in the back row leading the standing ovation at the curtain call.

He said he couldn't believe anybody could pull off playing his father but I had. No newspaper review ever meant as much.

A few weeks after the Toronto run, Josh and his wife, Kim Murdoch, came over to the house and Josh gave me a present. It was a large picture of Zero as Tevye. He told me it was Zero's favorite picture of himself taken during a rehearsal of Fiddler. Then he said, "Oh, but I have one criticism of the show."

"What's that?" I wanted to know.

He said, "You never once used Zero's favorite word."

I said, "Tell me what it is and I'll put it in"

Josh smiled and screamed, "COCKSUCKER!"

Josh Mostel told me his father's favorite word.

I had always wanted to play Sheridan Whiteside in *The Man Who Came To Dinner*. I thought it would be a wonderful fit and two of our *Zero Hour* producers, Dan Wackerman and Kevin Kennedy at The Theater at Saint Clements, were presenting it. They asked me if I would play Whiteside and of course I accepted immediately. My Lorraine Sheldon was the brilliant Tony Award winner Cady Huffman. I unashamedly adore Miss Huffman. In the play, Lorraine Sheldon is taken out of the home in an Egyptian sarcophagus. On the night of our first preview, I came offstage and stood in the wings ready to go out and take my bow. I stood next to Cady who said, "By the way, I have a piece of advice for you." Now usually when one actor says to the other, "I have a piece of advice for you," it's not going to end well. Actors just don't give other actors notes. Period. So I trepidatiously said, "Yes, and what's that?" She said, "Never cut a fart in a closed sarcophagus!" If I didn't adore her then I adored her even more after.

Above; Me with Cady Huffman
Below; With Kaufman and Hart (Ann and Christopher, children of the authors.

I was only the fourth man ever to play Sheridan Whiteside in New York City, following in the footsteps of Monty Woolley, Ellis Rabb and the marvelous Nathan Lane. I thought it would be a wonderful fit and I could slip easily into the part but boy was it a challenge. No doubt the toughest role I ever played. But I got to work with Kaufman and Hart. Their children that is. Anne Kaufman, daughter of George S., and Christopher Hart (son of Moss) were a big part of the production. They were very enthusiastic about what I was bringing to the part and to have their approval meant the world to me.

Sheridan Whiteside, based on the acerbic New York Times critic Alexander Woolcott, is a very compelling character. He's nasty, critical, haughty, insulting and a general pain in the ass the audience has to love. Our first couple of previews were very rough. The part is like *Hamlet* in that there's an enormous amount of lines to learn. But after a week that show purred.

After the first incarnation of *Zero Hour* closed in New York (yes, there would be a revival) I decided I wanted to write a show about my mentor and dear friend David Burns. He did so many shows and introduced me to so many of my favorite actors who became mentors that I thought this is a show I wanted to dedicate to all of them.

I called the show *Character Man* and it was a tribute to the men who contributed to making me who I was as a performer: Davy Burns, Jack Albertson, Lou Jacobi, Jack Gilford, Hans Conried and Barney Martin.

This show, unlike *Zero Hour,* was a joy to perform. Although there were some tearful moments there was no big drama in which I had to explode and it was enjoyable to sing ten songs that I loved singing. But *Character Man* had a very rough start.

It was 2012 and I had just finished writing the first draft of the show and was choosing the songs to include. Steve and I were doing a cruise from London to New York and we hit the worst storms in the history of sailing. Three hurricanes converged at one time and for four days we bobbed and weaved through thirty foot seas. The ship's entertainers were all seasick and the new entertainers who were supposed to join in Halifax couldn't because the port was closed. Paul McFarland, the ship's extraordinary cruise director, asked if I had another show I could do? I told him it was theoretical at that point but he didn't care. I was the last entertainer standing. *Character Man* was born on the *Crystal Symphony* in the middle of the Atlantic Ocean. Productions at Stages Rep in Houston and the Stage Door Theatre in Florida gave me my "out of town tryouts" for the show.

The New York production of Character Man at Urban Stages. Behind me are pictures of Zero, Davy and Jack Gilford.

shortly after we got back to New York Frances Hill, Artistic Director of Urban Stages, called to say she had heard about the show and was looking for one person musical. *Character Man*, directed by Robert Bartley, opened at the Urban Stages Theater on February 28, 2014 and once again, thankfully I was nominated for a Drama Desk Award for Outstanding Solo Show. This time John Douglas Thompson won, and deservedly so, for his brilliant portrayal of Louis Armstrong.

A few years ago, I got a call from our friends at The Theater St Clements asking me if I would like to revive *Zero Hour* for a few months. It had been years since I put on the mantle of Zero and was now older than Zero was when he died. I wasn't sure if I could pull it off eight years later.

But saying yes brought me one of the most indelible and memorable encounters of my life. The legendary Harold Prince came to the penultimate performance to do a talk back with me. Hal Prince, of course, is the great genius of the American theater responsible for so many musicals and no one has won more Tony Awards than he.

I had met Mr. Prince a few times socially, but nothing of substance - just casual encounters at different theatrical events. After, he couldn't have been more effusive about the play and about my performance. I couldn't believe that how Prince had put his hand on my shoulder and said to me, "Jim, you are a great artist. You're absolutely brilliant." (I made him write it on my Playbill too).

I felt like I had been knighted by the King himself. but he was only a prince.

My last performance of *Zero* took place at the Invisible theater in Tucson, Arizona in January of 2019. I had never been so sick in my life but got through the two performances and still I don't know how I did it. A phenomenon known as "Dr. Spotlight."

But at that point I realized it was time to hang up my "Zero" shoes. I was now ten years older than Mostel was when he died.

Also it takes a lot of strength to be on the stage for two hours without a break just talking and erupting.

Performing *Zero Hour* brought so many wonderful people into my life but none was more unexpected than Barbra Streisand. Early on during the Los Angeles production a wonderful man named Gary Smith offered to bring the show to New York. Gary was a veteran of so many TV shows, the Director of the Tonys and the Oscars and countless specials, he is one of the most respected men in the business and rightly so. Gary and his talented artist wife Maxine were best friends with Jim Brolin and his wife Barbra.

Gary, who was a close friend of Zero, was moved by the show and invited "The Brolins" to come see it. We were all very excited the night that six tickets were put aside in the back of the house but she was rehearsing her concert tour and decided at the last minute not to come.

Gary asked me if it would be OK if he set up two cameras in the back and recorded the show and presented it to Barbara that way. I had no objections and so the camera shoot was set. About three weeks later Gary told me that he, Maxine, Barbra and Jim had been on vacation together and *Zero Hour* was the main entertainment.

He told me during the first fifteen minutes Barbra was kind of itchy and not paying much attention. Then when Zero talks about the blacklist, she was hooked and loved the show. This engendered an invitation to see her concert in Fort Lauderdale. I was to fly down, get an all access pass, meet Miss Streisand and hang out. The invitation itself was almost surreal. She was performing in Fort Lauderdale at the Bell Center, a seventeen thousand seat arena, and it was the day that she was shooting the closeups for the DVD of the show.

Barbra appeared on stage at two-thirty in the afternoon and sang until six-thirty. And I knew she still had a three hour concert to go and was amazed she was singing full out. At the break, Gary brought me backstage and introduced me to Barbra. She gushed, "There you are, I'm a fan. You're such a good actor. I love the show. Who wrote the play?" I told her I wrote it myself. That seemed to shock her and she kept saying, "What? You wrote it too? My God, you're so brilliant."

Well her concert was terrific. She sang for almost three hours. There was an incident when an audience member started yelling some unpleasantness directed at her.

During the day there were huge signs posted all over the Bell Center that the taking of pictures was absolutely forbidden. But still I had my little camera in my pocket and I couldn't resist . After all I had an all access pass and maybe people thought that I was part of the show just doing a job.

Sadly, the pictures came out very fuzzy but (as you can see) I include one here. After the show we went back to hang out in her dressing room. There was only six of us there. I was standing next to her when she brought up the heckler. Barbra said, "Hey did you hear during the concert somebody yelled out, 'Barbra you're a bitch.'" I took a chance and I said, "Yes, that was me." She looked at me for a moment and then just broke up. She said, "You're funny too."

I was desperate to have a picture taken with her but a few minutes before I was about to reach into my pocket and pull out the camera. her security knocked on the door. A security man who was the size of a walk in refrigerator, said, "Miss Streisand, we found the person who's been taking pictures of you all afternoon." My heart sank. I have been caught. Oh my God, what had started out to be a wonderful encounter was now going to be the most embarrassing moment of my life.

She said, "Oh, yeah? Who was it?" The guard answered that it was somebody who was part of her entourage. My heart sank even further. I had my hand on my camera and was about pull it out, confess and throw myself on the mercy of the court.

Just as I was about to confess and throw myself on the mercy of the court, he said, "It was the lady who was your stand in." I said, "How dare she!" Well at that point I was too afraid to ask for a picture because I thought I would reveal myself so I asked if she would give me her autograph. She took one of the very expensive programs, I think they were $40 a shot, and wrote on the front of it. "Jim, You're Terrific! And the show. My best to you - Barbra."

With Piper Laurie, the director of *Zero Hour,* at Sardi's on the opening night.

As Zero Mostel

CHAPTER TWELVE
Broadway and Beyond

The original cast of *Something's Afoot*. That's me on the bottom in old age makeup. Now I don't need any to look old.

So many of my dreams have come true over the years, but the biggest dream has escaped me. I have never originated a part or done a run in a Broadway show. The closest I came was playing Flint in the pre-Broadway tryout of *Something's Afoot*. I had been doing the part since the inception of the show, including all the backer's auditions as well as the Alliance Theatre and Goodspeed Opera House productions.

When the original director was fired, his replacement thought I was too young for the part, didn't like the heavy make-up I was wearing and decided to recast the part with an actor of the right age. It was a blow but I thought one day I would be on Broadway.

Well, even though I've never done a long run I have appeared on Broadway several times in some very special one-night only productions. Charlotte Moore and Ciaran O'Reilly of the Irish Rep Company asked me to play Andrew McLaren in their benefit production of *Brigadoon* at the Shubert Theatre starring Tony winners Len Cariou and Christine Ebersole. The next year it was back to the Shubert for Oliver! opposite my pal Brian Stokes Mitchell who proved to be a brilliant Fagin. The

With Brian Stokes Mitchell, Melissa Errico and James Barbour in the Irish Rep's performance of *Oliver!* at the Shubert Theatre.

production of *Oliver!* was not a pain-free experience.

The day before the show I dislocated my shoulder but wasn't about to let it stop me from appearing on a Broadway stage. I was playing Mr. Brownlow, Oliver's long lost grandfather, and was worried about the final scene. Our director, Charlotte Moore, had the stagehands set a bench for me so that Oliver could run into my arms while I was seated and I could embrace him with a non-pain inducing hug. At the performance that night, the stagehands forgot the bench, Oliver came running out from the wings, jumped into my arms and the pain was almost exquisite. The tears flowed down my cheeks leaving the audience thinking that I was overwhelmed by the reunion. Now, that's acting.

Performing on the stage of a Broadway theater is like no other thrill the world because you are not standing there alone. You stand with every great performer who stood there before and you can feel their ghosts loving support around you. Here I was performing on the same stage where I saw Jackie Gleason

"Never Too Late To Fall In Love" with Harvey Evans at the Al Hirschfeld Theatre.

in *Take Me Along*, Vivian Leigh in *Ivanov*, Barbra Streisand in *I Can Get It For You Wholesale* and Anthony Newley in *Stop The World I Want To Get Off*. They were singing along with me.

Broadway Backwards is an annual theatrical event created by Robert Bartley, a brilliant choreographer and director. Bob directed my *Character Man* show and he asked me to appear in two editions of the show.

The premise of *Broadway Backwards* is that men perform songs originated by women and vice versa. The first time I did Broadway Backwards was at the Al Hirschfeld Theatre and the number was *Never Too Late To Fall In Love* from *The Boyfriend*. My dancing partner was the legendary Harvey Evans who had appeared in over fifteen Broadway shows.

The night of the performance was my night off from *Zero Hour* in Toronto and I had to fly in at the last minute to rehearse with Harvey and the orchestra. We put some simple staging together, did a run-through and then left the rest to adrenaline as we debuted our number in front of a packed fourteen hundred seat house.

One of the dreams I've always had was to stop a show cold on Broadway and it happened that night. Harvey and I absolutely brought the house down. One of the other performers doing *Broadway Backwards* was the fabulous Patricia Morison, the star of the original production of *Kiss Me, Kate*. Pat was appearing on her 100th birthday and she sang *Brush Up Your Shakespeare*, Cole Porter's tongue twisting comedy number. She was superb. She belted out the song sitting in a wheelchair, hit every note, got every laugh and when she was done, I have never heard an ovation like that in my life. The audience cheered, they screamed, they stood on their feet and the applause must have gone on for at least two or three minutes which is an eternity for a standing ovation. The host of the evening, Julie White, came onstage for the next introduction. Finally, Patricia's ovation ended and Julie said, "Well, ladies and gentlemen our next performer is just fucked!"

I sat with Pat Morison at the afterparty. She turned to me very shyly and said, "Jimmy, did they applaud because I'm old?" I said, "No, darling. They applauded because you're a legend who knocked it out of the park tonight." She liked that.

At the *Broadway Backwards* afterparty with Broadway's original Kate, the enchanting Patricia Morison at age 100.

The evening was so successful that Bob Bartley wrote the next year's edition of *Broadway Backwards* to star Tony Sheldon and me. Tony is the Tony Award nominated star of *Priscilla, Queen of the Desert* and a cherished friend. The thought of working with him was irresistible but I had to make a choice.

I had been offered a six week run doing a new show at the Denver Theater Center that conflicted with *Broadway Backwards*, which was going to be performed at the fabled Palace Theatre. I would be one of the stars of the evening getting the last bow. I turned down six weeks of work because I thought that when I am on my deathbed, am I going to say, "Oh boy, I played the Denver

Theater Center" or "I played the Palace!" The choice was obvious.

That night, as I stood there for the final bow all I could think of was the ghosts who stood in that same spot so many years before – Judy Garland, Ethel Merman, Sophie Tucker, Burns and Allen, Jack Benny, W.C. Fields and so many more. I
might have not done a run but sure enough, I got to stop the show. I don't know if that dream of originating a part or doing a Broadway run will ever come true. As I write

The last bow at The Palace Theatre with Tony Sheldon and Stephanie J. Block

this I'm seventy-four years old and I don't know if I have the steam to do eight shows a week anymore but who knows – actors are ever optimistic.

One of the great bonuses of being a performer is to be invited to work in exotic, foreign venues that you dreamed about but never thought you would see. In 1995, our friends Adam and Nicky Wright, who we met on the *Galileo* so many years before, were now the Cruise

Director and Social Hostess for the Orient Lines on their ship, the Marco Polo.

After my book about Lucy came out, Adam contacted me and said, "You're an author now. Do you want to come out and do a cruise with us and talk about some of the stars you've met?" I thought what a wonderful way to see the world and accepted immediately. A few weeks later, Steve and I flew to Bangkok for three days and then to Singapore to join the ship.

Ships and sailing had always been a very important part of my life; all my cruises with dad and meeting Steve on a ship.

The first thing I remember about my new avocation as a cruise ship lecturer is getting off the plane in Singapore and my eyeglasses totally fogged up. humidity was like stepping into a sauna, literally. Our first stop was the Raffles Hotel where I felt like David Niven sipping my Sloe Gin Fizz. Above our heads were rattan fans slowly moving back and forth to stir the moist air. Although these fans were now operated electrically, we were told that young boys used to sit over the diners fanning them manually.

Then the *Marco Polo* docked in the Philippines where Adam and Nicky and Steve and I were unceremoniously thrown out of the Manila Hotel. We were talking to some bellman in the lobby and he said that the great General Douglas MacArthur had commanded the Pacific fleet from his penthouse on the fifth floor. Sometimes it was open to visitors. We asked if we could see it and the desk clerk told us that the room had been rented and that the guests were arriving momentarily. The four of us looked at each other and decided we would take a chance before the guest got there and up we went to the forbidden room. Sure enough, the suite was open.

Steve had the video camera recording while Adam, Nicky and I explored the rooms. This apartment is where all the American presidents and other world leaders stayed when they were in Manila. We were taking pictures and touring the rooms when we heard a voice. "What are you doing here?" I turned to see a short man in a white server's jacket yelling at me. I lied and said, "The desk clerk told us we could come up and look around." He said, "You lie! You're a liar. They did not tell you that. People are coming. You get out. GET OUT!" Oh well, we'd been thrown out of better places.

We had a three day stopover on the island of Bali where Adam and Nicky knew of a hotel where we could spend a few nights off the ship. It was called the Hotel Serai and it rested on a pure white sand beach framed against the deep blue of the Indian Ocean. The peace and quiet were profound. The only sound was a soft, "whoosh, whoosh, whoosh" and we looked to see the young hotel gardeners

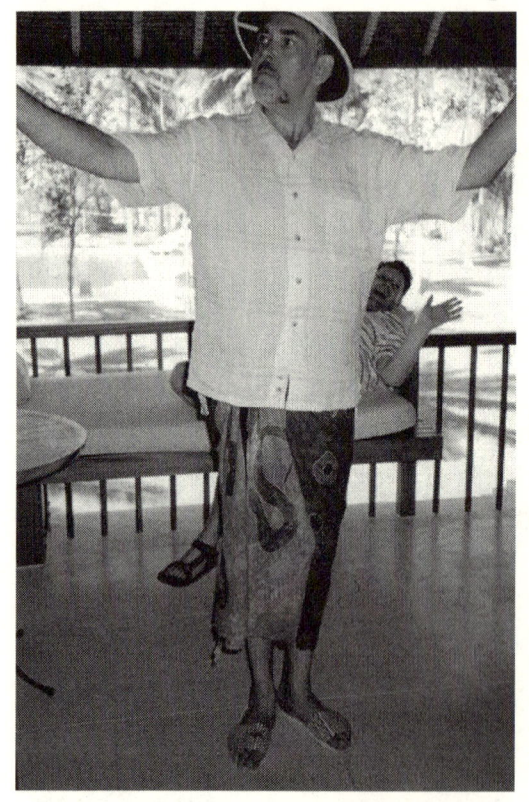

Exploring Bali with my new Pith Helmet and Sarong. I'm on the balcony where I slept al fresco with unwanted friends.

squatting on the lawn cutting the grass, not with mowers, but machetes. Each cut produced the "whoosh."

Adam and Nicky had been to Bali many times before and they knew of a little village that they thought we would enjoy seeing. It was a community of some two hundred Balinese families who lived with no electricity. The only running water was a nearby spring where they filled their pots and jars to drink and cook over an open fire. They began their day when the sun rose and slept when it set.

It wasn't a touristy place at all. They had a little stand set up in the front of the village for tourists to buy their handmade souvenirs but we came in the back way where it was truly experiencing something from another world. We watched the village women carry their laundry baskets on their head and go to the fast-running stream so that they could wash the clothes against the rocks. The people were beyond friendly. One man we met insisted we visit his house and meet his wife and child. The "house" had no walls, but rather a large open covered space with mats for beds and cushions to sit. What struck me was how happy these people were. Though they had absolutely no modern conveniences, they were filled with joy and loved their life. Before we left our new friend's house, he brought out a tray of tapestries and sarongs his wife had woven. We left the village with fond memories, warm hearts and a bag full of sarongs.

That night I decided to sleep under the stars on the balcony of our room. Being a city boy, I had never slept under the stars before. When I woke up the next morning, there were scads of birds flying over my head. When the waiter brought the breakfast, he asked if we had slept well? I told him it was a great sleep and fun to wake up with the sparrows. He giggled and said, "No sir, they're BATS!"

Steve was very sick on the trip. His health was deteriorating rapidly. When we disembarked the *Marco Polo* in Hong Kong, Steve wanted to have a blue blazer made by a Hong Kong tailor. A master tailor delivered the jacket over night and when Steve tried it on, he said, "Perfect fit, sir. And you will wear this jacket for ten years." It jolted us back to reality because we both knew that at that time, he didn't have ten years.

Some people say there are no accidents but a very strange and unexpected encounter happened. About a day after we got back from Asia, we were in Ralph's Supermarket on Ventura Blvd. in Los Angeles and I ran into an old friend named Kirk Frederick. Kirk had worked as a costume coordinator for my pal Charles Pierce, the female impersonator.

Mountains of ice in Antarctica.

We bumped into him in Aisle Six: Jams and Jellies. He said, "Oh, you're so tan. Where have you been?" I told him I been lecturing on a cruise ship in Asia. He asked what the topics of my lectures were? I told him I talked about the Golden Age of Hollywood: Lucy, Kate Hepburn and Ginger. I then asked him if he was still doing costumes? He said, "No, I book the lecture program for Crystal Cruises."

The next day we had tickets for an Alaska Cruise onboard the *Crystal Harmony*. Crystal Cruises is an absolute top of the line luxury brand. One cruise led to another and now as I write this it has been 25 years since I began working with Crystal. Steve and I would do about three or four cruises a year when we could and it has taken us to all over the world. At this writing we have been to eighty-four countries and all seven continents. We were in Antarctica and I thought I would smell the most pristine air I've ever enjoyed in my life. The air was crisp and cold but not freezing. New York has seen colder temperatures than we were experiencing that January approaching Elephant Island. But the smell was overwhelming. I couldn't fathom where this odor attack was coming from until I asked one of the crew who had done the trip several times. He said, "Oh, it's penguin guano." We looked over at one of the mountains of ice thinking that the black specks were rocks. Until they started to move. Who would have thought that Beijing smelled better than Antarctica.

Steve has a theory that cruising is like visiting a nudist colony. Everyone's equal. You never know who you are going to sit next to on a ship. It could be a multimillionaire or person who has saved up their whole life for one trip.

One of the stars I worked with on the *Crystal Serenity* was Jack Jones. It was a Hawaii cruise and Jack and I were both performing. When we got to Honolulu, Jack invited several of the performers to go to the Waikiki Beachcomber Hotel and see his friend, Don Ho.

Don Ho sat in a wicker throne in front of an audience of two hundred adoring fans. On the desk in front of him was a lineup of ten drinks and a phone to call the bar in case he needed refills. By the end of the evening he was snockered.

But I have never seen any performer hold the stage for almost three hours like he did – improvising, telling jokes, making the audience members get up and perform and singing "Tiny Bubbles" eighteen times. Mr. Ho invited Jack, *The Phantom of the Opera* star Dale Kristien and I to perform and afterwards, Don spent as much time with every member of the audience who wanted to meet him and take a photo. It was truly a remarkable event. A great entertainer that, Mr Ho.

At the Waikiki Beachcomber Hotel with Dale Kristien, the extraordinary Don Ho and Jack Jones.

By way of a wonderful coincidence, when *The Last Session* was opening in London Steve and I were scheduled to do a transatlantic crossing from London to New York on the *Crystal Symphony*. We planned to get there a few days before the sailing to watch rehearsals.

Our friend Rich Bloch was going to be in London at the same time. What follows is the adventure we called "The Great London Hotel Caper" where I pulled off one of the greatest di-dos of all time. (I hope the hotel chain is not reading).

I found a Four-star hotel on Priceline for $129.00 a night. When I paid in advance I was given the name of the hotel, which was indeed four stars and centrally located on the River Thames.

I once kept a blind email account that appeared to be a public relations firm from New York City. I then invented a fictitious woman named Donna Court Thorne, head of the agency, who only had one client…me.

Then I found out the name of the PR person that represented the hotel we booked, wrote to them (as Donna) and told them that her client (me) was coming to London for the opening of his show in the West End and any courtesy that could be shown would be greatly appreciated. The return email to Ms. Thorne emphasized how happy the hotel was to host her celebrity client.

Rich booked the same hotel so we could be together and arrived at the hotel very early on the day before we did. His room wasn't ready. The clerk said he could come back and check in at 3:00 o'clock. He asked what he could do until it was available and the clerk said, "We have a very comfortable lobby."

The next morning Steve and I arrived at the hotel and called Rich to join us in the lobby. Rich watched as I gave my name to the desk clerk and the guy almost did a backflip. "Oh, Mr. Brochu. We've been expecting you and are so happy you're here. Thank you for staying with us. Now your room is not ready yet but we have another room where you can refresh and change until your own room is ready." Rich looked like he was going to fall through the floor.

We went to our "changing room" which would have been just fine, then two hours later we got a call that our room was ready. By this time I had let Rich in on the secret of how we got the upgrade. We went up to the new room, opened the door and found ourselves in the Presidential Suite: champagne and chocolates, dining room, bedrooms, marble bath, full kitchen and a living room with floor to ceiling windows overlooking the Thames, featuring a spectacular view of Westminster Palace and Big Ben. All for $129.00 a night.

In 2012, Bret Bullock, who was Vice President of Entertainment at Crystal Cruises asked me to transition from being a ship's lecturer to a headline entertainer. I did a tab version of *Zero Hour* which brought us two extraordinary adventures: Egypt and China.

For the Egypt cruise we flew first to India to pick up the ship in Mumbai, which provided a very unwanted, nerve-racking experience – almost missing the ship. Our flight to Singapore was delayed three hours and when we finally arrived in Mumbai (once Bombay) there was no one to meet us. We were offered two taxis: a regular cab for $9 but if we wanted air conditioning, it would be $10. Boy, did we want the air conditioning.

We took a very small, ancient, rickety cab with the luggage tied on the top. We asked the driver if he knew where the Cruise Ship Terminal was and he assured us though an excessive number of bows and grunts that he did. Except he spoke no English and he would have assured us he knew the entire Gettysburg Address by heart. The drive through Mumbai was exciting, frightening, eye popping, unsettling and unforgettable.

The streets were teaming with cars, bicycles, tuk-tuks and thousands of people packing the streets: all the women were wearing a rainbow of colorful saris. We were moving at about five miles an hour, getting more nervous, going nowhere, in the car over an hour with about a half hour left to catch the ship.

We finally decided to pull over to find a policeman to see if he could help. But the officer, while cordial, spoke no English and had no idea what we were talking about. Just then, Steve looked out the window and saw the sign, Mumbai Cruise Terminal. We had stumbled on the place without even noticing it. Needless to say the Cruise Director was very happy that we made the ship with ten minutes to spare.

Unlike the Panama Canal with its' locks and levels, the Suez Canal is absolutely level with no locks and endless miles of sand on either side: Egypt to the left, Israel on the right when traveling North. We took a two-hour bus ride from Port Said to Luxor, the Valley of the Kings. During the whole trip we had an empty escort bus that was there in case our bus broke down, but we found out later there were four men armed with rifles just in case anybody got the idea to kidnap the tourists.

In Luxor, which was probably the hottest place I've ever experienced in my life, we got to visit the tomb of King Tut. As we went down into the chamber, we were astonished to see the wall paintings were still as vibrant and colorful as the day they were painted three thousand years before. The guide explained that the paintings had never been touched and the preservation was due to the dryness of the tomb. When we got to the pyramids in Giza, if you turned the wrong way all you would see is the backside of Cairo with Kentucky Fried Chicken and McDonald's signs peppering the landscape.

We were overwhelmed by the great structures and if I wasn't so claustrophobic I would have joined Steve who crawled inside. Then we ran into one of the world weary, rich ladies from the ship who looked at the Sphinx, shrugged and said, "Eh, not so much."

I was one of two celebrity entertainers on board the *Crystal Serenity* for the trip to China in 2012. My fellow headline entertainer was Regis Philbin who, I'm sorry to say, turned out to be one of the most obnoxious, egotistical and unpleasant individuals I have ever encountered. On the first day at sea, I introduced myself to him as one of his fellow entertainers. He looked at my outstretched hand and said, "So?" He was also totally rude to the crew, stand-offish with the passengers and his wife only spoke up to complain.

All Regis was required to do was one forty-five minute presentation about his new book. He spoke for twenty-five minutes and said he would leave twenty minutes for pictures with the guests afterwards. About three quarters of the audience lined up to get a photo with "Rege," but as soon as the twenty minutes was up. He said, "Sorry" walked away and left about fifteen people without their photo. I mean, come on. Can't you spend five extra minutes to make a few people happy? I found out later that Regis asked to return for a cruise the next year and the company politely said, "No, thanks."

China was astonishing. I had imagined the "old" China, thinking we would get there and people would be running around in Mao jackets and pulling rickshaws. After passing Hermes, Rolex, Chanel, Dolce and Gabbana and every other high-end store you could imagine, we arrived in front of the ultra-modern New World Hotel. Everyone on the street was sharply dressed and very sophisticated. The architecture of the skyscrapers was ultra-modern and cutting edge.

Our first stop was Shanghai where the fog and the smog were so thick that when they took us up to the top of the tallest building to take in the view, all they could show us was a panoramic picture of what the city looked like beneath the smog. However Beijing was a totally different story with clear skies and crisp, beautiful air. The two highlights of the trip were the mandatory visit to the Great Wall of China and then a dinner for all of the passengers at the Great Hall of the People.

It was thrilling to sit in the same room where Nixon and Mao once toasted each other and began the thaw in Sino-American relations. The Great Hall is an enormous room, probably the size of an indoor football field. architecturally remarkable in that there are no beams or supports to the ceiling.

Our guide told us that Communism in China was like an apple: the outer skin is communist but it was very capitalistic at its core. He was very open about what was going on in the country until we got to Tiananmen Square. I asked him where the incident with the tank had happened so many years before. His eyes darted around \ the square and then he said, "We can talk about that on the bus." All of a sudden I felt there were a thousand eyes on us.

While we were taking a tour of the Forbidden City, home of the Chinese Emperors, I had to sit down to rest for a few minutes and as I

My caricature on a plate from the Al Hirschfeld of The People's Republic.

was about to stand up Steve shouted at me, "Sit still." Of course I couldn't imagine what he was talking about and I started to get up again. Again he shouted, "Just sit still!"

I looked over to see that there was a puffy-faced Chinese man with a plate in one hand and a marker in the other doing a sketch of me. When he finished he brought it over to show me the finished drawing. He handed it to me, smiled and uttered the two English words he knew, "Ten dollars."

Steve and I were in Paris on July 26, 1991 which was the final day of that year's Tour De France. An old friend of Steve's lived in Paris and we called to see if he was in town. His friend was named Olivier, a flight attendant for Air France, and he had the weekend off.

Olivier was very excited that Steve and I were in town and he drove over to our hotel to pick us up for his private tour of the city. Olivier and his friend Jose came to the hotel driving an Austin-America car that was something you didn't get into but rather put on. We squeezed into a tiny tin can on wheels and zipped around the streets of Paris.

We started in Montmartre at the Sacre Coeur Basilica where we lit candles for our family and friends, took in the Picasso Museum and then Olivier decided he wanted to show us the Arc de Triomphe and so we headed for the Champs Elysée.

Olivier made a right turn passed some barricades and all of a sudden we're driving down the middle of the wide boulevard. But there was something not usual – there were no other cars, thousands of people lining both sides of us cheering and waving. Olivier realized too late that the crowd had not assembled because they heard we were in town. The climax of the Tour de France was minutes away.

There was no place to turn off, so down the Champs Elysée we drove, one lone car. I kept thinking this is what it must have been like on that day in 1944 when Paris was liberated from the Nazis and the crowds gathered on that same street to cheer for the American troops

On a South American cruise we met a fellow entertainer named Shirley Dominguez a virtuoso of the harp. Shirley had a beach house just outside of Montevideo and when we docked there she invited all the entertainers to join her and her family for a typical Uruguayan barbecue.

Her beach house was steps from the Ocean, and when our group of strolling players arrived her mother and father, who spoke no English, were barbecuing what looked like a side of beef with enough food to feed the Argentinian army.

Shirley told us that one of the activities she had arranged for after lunch was horseback riding. When I was a kid my uncle John took me for a horseback ride and I got thrown. It was a

Carmen and me.

very painful experience that knocked the wind out of me and made me terrified of horses although I had always loved them from afar. I decided that this was the day I was going to conquer my fear and go for a horseback ride.

A delightful man who looked like "El Exigente" arrived with ten beautiful horses and we all chose one to mount. I chose the biggest, fattest one because I was huge at the time and I didn't want the horse to get hurt. I was wearing my white beard and the owner of the horse saw me and said warmly, "Ah! Mr. Hemingway! Nice to have you." I joked that I wasn't Ernest Hemingway but just as good a writer.

He helped me on the horse which was enormous and we went for a wonderful ride. I sheepishly rode out like Don Knotts in *The Shakiest Gun In The West* but came back a half hour later like Roy Rogers thundering into a rodeo at full gallop. My horse was absolutely wonderful, sweet and gentle.

As I was dismounting, the lovely owner of the horse came over. I told him I had a great ride and asked the horse's name. He startled me when he said, "Carmen!" I told him I thought it was a guy horse. "No," he said, "and she's going to have a baby soon, maybe today!"

Then he thought for a minute, looked at my white beard and said, "Yes! We'll call the new horse Hemmingway!"

I first met Marge Champion briefly in 1964 when Davy was doing *Hello, Dolly!* and she would come backstage to give notes on behalf of the show's director, her husband Gower Champion.

Marge and Gower were one of the most celebrated dance teams of the 40's and 50's until Gower became one of Broadway's most sought-after directors. Steve and

Marge and I lived in the same apartment complex in Manhattan when we got to be closer many years later.

Ironically, we were booked to do a cruise together in 2002 from London to New York with stops in Iceland and Canada. When the ship docked in St. John's, Newfoundland, a place that none of us had ever been before, we disembarked the ship to face a very steep, San Francisco-like hill. Marge said, "Come on, let's go for a walk and see what's there." We had celebrated her eighty-third birthday the night before and yet she wanted to climb the hill and I didn't think I could make it.

Once again, she said, "Come on. You guys can do it! It'll be good exercise." And with that challenge, she started up the hill. We were not about to let her go by herself so we begrudgingly and breathlessly trudged up the hill panting behind her.

St. John's is a quiet, quaint seaside town with colorfully painted houses and populated with some of the friendliest people in the world. When the three of us finally got to the top of the hill, we looked around to see where we were. Then Steve spotted the street sign and found that Marge had unexpectedly led us to a street whose name made us all smile. Marge had led us up the hill to *Gower Street*. Marge and Gower were together again. At this writing Marge, who was born the same year as my mother, recently turned a hundred and one and is living back in California near her children.

Traveling has become one of our passions but the best part of it is coming home. Home for us now is back in my hometown, New York City. We live in a wonderful building that was established in the 1970's for actors and artist. Back then nobody wanted to live in Hell's Kitchen but now it seems to be "the place." When we moved back to New York, my friend and director, Piper Laurie, introduced us to a man who became one of our closest friends, Robert Osborne of Turner Classic Movies.

Bob was one of the classiest, wittiest, most wonderful human beings one could ever have in their life. He was loyal to a fault, excessively funny and had style beyond measure. We would spend many hours together laughing, talking about old movies and then laughing some more.

Steve and I love giving parties and it was always fun when Bob would say, "Can I bring a friend?" Of course the answer was always yes because you never knew who is going to walk in the door with him. Yes, he arrived one night with Angela Lansbury on his arm.

When Bob died in 2017, I went through my emails and found I had saved one hundred and three from him. I'm reprinting the one he sent us when we moved into our building because it's typical of many of the emails I got from Bob. Funny, gossipy and literate.

Jim,
Thinking about you daily. Sorry I'm been so silent. It comes not from a natural timidity but the total loss of a voice. I suspect it may have to do with a recent immersion in silent screen stars for a Turner project. But please know you're on my mind, I send you big

hugs and much affection and I have NO IDEA how Cameron Diaz became a movie star so please don't ask

I hope you're enjoying your new digs. I have great affection for that building. It's where I used to stay with a friend when I'd visit NYC in the 1970s and 1980s and once on my way there after seeing a play and having a late dinner had my first glimpse of Lauren Bacall when I was walking across 43rd Street about one a.m. and heard her scream "I just want you to FUCK ME!!!" She was on her knees on a deserted parking lot trying to hold onto Harry Guardino who was trying to get away from her. Luckily, I was the only one on the street that night. Only later was I told West 43rd between 8th & 9th at that time was dangerous to even walk briskly on. It certainly was for Harry.

xxox
-- Robert O.

Bob was classy to the end. His last words were, "See you at the after party." I'm grateful that we will always have Bob on television with all his wonderful introductions to the great films that he loved. A very, very special man.

One of the most unexpected pleasures that's appeared this late in life is finding a whole new audience doing cabaret. Michael Feinstein, who I've known since the Earth was cooling, has a beautiful club in New York where I have performed more than two dozen times, sometimes solo and sometimes singing duets with folks like Stephen Schwartz, Anita Gillette and Marilyn Maye.

Singing with Marliyn Maye at Birdland and Anita Gilette at Feinstein's

I still love being on the stage although when theatres will reopen is anyone's guess. My last Off-Broadway appearance in Ed Kleban's show, *A Class Act,* only made it as far as a dress rehearsal. But I was appearing with seven of the most talented kids I've ever worked with and enjoying the camaraderie of a new cast. We were set to open on March 12th, the 49th anniversary of Davy's death, when at 4:00 o'clock that afternoon we were told not to come to the theater. New York had shut down. Broadway was closed. Everything stopped

As I write this we're living in a very strange time; the time of Covid, social distancing and masks; no theatres, few restaurants and certainly no cruises.

But my favorite Bible passage is, "This too shall pass." I know New York will come back and be the great booming city that it was a few years ago.

And then we will always have Sardi's to meet friends at the bar. Oh yes, that dream did come true. Sure enough on July 1, 2001 Max Klimavicius and Sean Ricketts who own Sardi's gave me that great honor. They

My last stage appearance in *A Class Act* with some awesomely talented young actors. We were supposed to open on March 12th and then....

put my caricature up in that empty space next to David Burns. I literally wept when I thought that he and I will be there on that wall together forever.

As for Steve, after thirty-five years it only gets better. We never officially married but took our vows to each other in August of 2016 in Dublin, Ireland. Steve is more passionate about music now than ever and has written so many incredible songs over the years. In 2008, the Gay Men's Chorus of San Francisco did his song cycle piece, *New World Waking,* supported by a fifty piece orchestra, one hundred voice choir and Jennifer Holliday as the soloist. From Steve, whose health is superb now, I truly have known unconditional love and I hope I have given back some of the same. To say that I'm grateful for everything that's happened in my life is an understatement. The highs have been steep and the lows shallow. I really know how lucky I have been and I thank the forces of the universe or whatever powers that kicked in to bring me the life that I have lived. My life has been a terrific ride. I'm not sure about an afterlife, but if do I meet God, the first thing I would say to him is, "Hello, sir. Can I go again?"

SPECIAL THANKS AND LOVE TO THE PEOPLE WHO HAVE SHARED MY LIFE

Peter Filichia, Linda Romanelli Leahy and Rob Leahy, Jane Goldman, Kate Leahy, Rich and Sue Bloch, Michael and Rachel Bloch, Madeline and Jerry Kane, David Gersten, Jenna and Chris Bates, Quinn Bates, Bill and Serena Brochu, Joan Brochu McGorry, Heidi and Tom Sullivan, Bill Miller, Ken Fallin, Kenn McLaughlin, Ed Decker, Louise Hirschfeld, Jane Klain, Brother Giles Turbee, Brother Gene Graham, Magda Katz, Mark Evanier, Merrill Stone, Jeramiah Peay, Phil Geoffrey Bond, Carl D. White, George A. McKay, Max Klimavicius, Sean Ricketts, Piper Laurie, Keith Cox, David Rambo and Ted Heyck, Scott Douglas, Jim Jimirro, Stan Freeman, Mort Schwartz, Eleanor Albano, Michael Sugar, Rob Schneider, Robert Cuccioli, Richard Bell, Jimmy Rilley, Marilyn Maye, Matt Murphy, Anita Gillette, Bill Goffi, Ken and Lynne Rees, Bob Levitt, Bernie and Joanne Furshpan, Bret Bullock, Charles Busch, Billy Stritch, Donna McKechnie, Russ Thomas Grieve, Shane Morley, Rick Spath, Paul and Pam McFarland, Gary and Maxine Smith, Jason Hungerford, Kirk Frederick, Jennifer De Chiara, Jacqueline Babbin, Michael Ehrman and Michael Lasswell.

Made in the USA
Middletown, DE
29 October 2020